TO ORDER MORE COPIES OF THIS BOOK

OR TO SEE A COMPLETE CATALOG OF FATHER CORAPI'S MATERIAL; BOOKS, CDS, DVDS, ETC. GO TO:

www.fathercorapi.com

OR
CALL TOLL FREE
1-888-800-7084

OR
US MAIL
SANTA CRUZ MEDIA, INC
PO BOX 550
WHITEFISH, MT, 59937

FATHER JOHN CORAPI SOLT, STD
CURRICULUM VITAE

Personal Data

Date of Birth: 20 May, 1947

Place of Birth: Hudson, New York

Ecclesiastical Status: Perpetually professed priest in good standing with the Society of Our Lady of the Most Holy Trinity, P.O. Box 152, Robstown, TX 78380, (361) 387-2754.

Academic Credentials

-Doctor of Sacred Theology (S.T.D.) awarded Magna cum Laude, Ecclesiastical Faculty Of Theology, University of Navarre, Pamplona, Spain. Thesis: The Cross of Christ in the Magisterium of John Paul II.

-Licentiate in Sacred Theology (S.T.L.) awarded Summa cum Laude, Ecclesiastical Faculty of Theology, University of Navarre, Pamplona, Spain, concentration in Dogmatic Theology.

-Master's Degree (M.A.) with highest honors in Sacred Scripture, Holy Apostles College And Seminary, Cromwell, Connecticut.

-Bachelor of Sacred Theology (S.T.B.) awarded Summa cum Laude, Ecclesiastical Faculty Of Theology, University of Navarre, Pamplona, Spain, concentration in Dogmatic Theology.

-Bachelor of Business Administration (B.B.A.), Pace University, Pleasantville, New York.

Holy Orders

Ordained transitional deacon 26 May, 1990 by His Excellency, Bishop Rene Gracida, Diocese of Corpus Christi, Texas for service to the Society of Our Lady of the Most Holy Trinity.

Ordained priest 26 May, 1991 by His Holiness, Pope John Paul II, St. Peter's Basilica, Vatican City.

Ecclesiastical Status

Perpetually professed priest in good standing with the Society of Our Lady of the Most Holy Trinity, a society of apostolic life of the diocesan rite with headquarters in Robstown, Texas.

Pastoral Experience

-Parish work, St. Marys' parish, Hudson, New York.

-Parish work, St. Anthony's parish, Robstown, Texas.

-Pastoral care of Mexican migrant farm workers.

-Director of Catholic Faith Formation, Diocese of Sacramento, California.

-Director of the Bishop's Project on the Catechism of the Catholic Church, Diocese of Sacramento, CA--Bishop William K. Weigand.

Present Work

-Preaching missions, retreats, and conferences throughout North America.

Published by Santa Cruz Media
©1996-2005 Santa Cruz Media, Inc
PO Box 550
Whitefish, MT 59937

ISBN-0-9773691-0-2
First printing, October, 2005

Ever Ancient...Ever New

(A collection of articles
on various subjects)

By Father John Corapi, SOLT, STD

Dedicated to His Holiness
John Paul the Great

Table of Contents

Introduction

Through this collection of articles, mostly written in mid 1990's, we hope to motivate people to a greater love for learning their Faith, which will lead them to a greater love for God, and a greater love for each other out of love for God.

The articles are mostly doctrinal in content, some of them conveying essential truths that are seldom seen in contemporary writing or preaching. The article on Divine Revelation, for example, reflects the teaching of the Church's Dogmatic Constitution on Divine Revelation, an extremely important document of the Second Vatican Council, yet nearly unknown to the Catholic faithful. I asked 1,000 active Catholics what it was and what it basically said. Only 12 out of 1,000 had even heard of it. This is indicative of the poor level of knowledge of the Catholic faith in the United States. This is, of course, a function of the teaching given, which is negligible in most cases.

To know our faith is to begin to know the Lord Jesus. To know Him is to love Him.

The article on forming and voting a Catholic conscience was read by over one million Catholics before the 2004 presidential election, and not without effect, as the outcome indicated.

We hope that by reading these brief and straight-forward articles people of good will might come to know their Faith, and in so doing come to know, love, and serve God so that they might be happy with Him in Heaven for all eternity.

Chapter One
Form Your Conscience,
Vote Your Conscience!

Every four years we enjoy a very great privilege, one that carries with it an equally great responsibility: that of voting for the officials who will govern the country and affect the lives of tens of millions of people, for better or for worse. Good government and just laws are not optional if the human family is to survive, much less prosper.

The tired argument that is so often heard these days about the separation of Church and State is a patently specious one, to say the least. The First Amendment of the Bill of Rights of the U.S. Constitution states:

Congress shall make no law respecting an establishment of religion, or prohibiting the free exercise thereof; or abridging the freedom of speech, or of the press; or the right of the people peaceably to assemble, and to petition the government for a redress of grievances.

The current erroneous interpretation of the separation of church and state is nothing less than an attack on the First Amendment of the Constitution of the United States of America itself.

Every citizen has a right to express their views and to vote in accordance with those views. The legitimate separation of church and state concerns the constitutional prohibition of one state sponsored religion, as well as the Founding Fathers' intent to keep the government out of the affairs of the various religions.

The version of separation of church and state that is presently being foisted on an unsuspecting public is tantamount to a suppression of the fundamental constitutional rights of a class of citizens. Since when is Christian thought not permitted to influence a country that was founded on Christian principles?

We share in the good and the evil of those we place in office. The Catechism of the Catholic Church teaches that, although "sin is a personal act, we have a responsibility for the sins committed by others when we cooperate in them" (CCC #1868). We can be accomplices in the sins of others:

By participating directly and voluntarily in them;

By ordering, advising, praising, or approving them;

By not disclosing or not hindering them when we have an   obligation to do so; (emphasis author's)

By protecting evil-doers" (CCC #1868).

The Catechism is thus consistent with traditional Catholic teaching which held that there are nine ways we can be an accessory to another's sin:

1. By counsel. I.e., "I think you should have an abortion; go ahead and have the abortion. It will help preserve your lifestyle."

2. By command. I.e., Telling your child, your friend, or your co-worker, "Have an abortion, you may lose your job if you don't."

3. By consent. I.e., "If you and your partner feel it's the best thing, go ahead and have a sexual relationship, get married. even if you're both of the same sex, etc. It's nobody's business."

4. By provocation. I.e., "Have the abortion! Aren't you in charge of your own life? The Pope is old and sick and who cares what he says anyhow."

5. By praise or flattery. I.e., "Oh, Senator, you are so courageous and kind in defending a woman's 'right' to an abortion."

6. By concealment. I.e., The pastor allows the senator, judge, president, etc. who has voted for, or otherwise promoted, abortion, euthanasia, human cloning, same-sex marriage, etc. to appear to be in good standing, when, in fact, they have caused grave public scandal by their actions. When the sin is public, the redress must be public. Although, I don't disagree with the courageous bishops who would deny such persons Communion, I do believe that the "confrontation" should take place, without question, long before they arrive at the altar rail.

7. By participation. I.e., "I'll drive you to the clinic. You need that abortion to be able to continue your lifestyle."

8. By silence. I.e., You refuse to speak out against what is a clear violation of human rights, an incredible persecution and prejudice against a class of human beings (the unborn). You hide

behind the Supreme Court's unjust and inherently illicit decision on abortion, saying it's the law of the land, when in fact it is the subversion and perversion of authentic law. The Nazi SS officers tried for war crimes used a similar defense, saying they were only following orders. They hung them, guilty as charged!

9. By defense of the evil. I.e., "It prevents child abuse by eliminating unwanted children; Women are more in charge of their lives, more liberated; it's so much more sophisticated and educated a thing to do, "etc. etc.

This year, more than ever, Catholics, and the entire human family, face a daunting challenge. We have to elect a president and other high ranking officials, and the choice could be a matter of life or death for the nation. For Catholics, it is a matter of a moral mandate: form your conscience so that you can vote your well-formed conscience. It is not morally permissible to merely vote for whomever you like based on superficial or even personal preferences. The candidates have to be evaluated in the sober and pure light of truth. Your conscience must be formed to the objective norm of that truth, which is Church teaching in faith and morals.

Since a physician needs to be concerned with what's sick, let's get right to the point. It is not morally possible for any Catholic to support abortion, euthanasia, fetal stem cell research, human cloning, or same-sex marriage. There are no ways around this, no justifications whatever. Why? For the simple reason that the Church holds these things to be intrinsically evil. They are evil in themselves, and no circumstances or subjective conditions can ever change that. They are not to be confused with such things as the death penalty and legitimate self-defense, which are not intrinsically evil, and which governments can, and often must, make use of. While the conditions for applying such unfortunate measures as the death penalty and waging war may be open to debate, they are not things evil in themselves, always and everywhere.

Any appeal to conscience concerning intrinsically evil matters is a specious one. Conscience is not an independent entity; it does not operate in a vacuum. Conscience must be formed to the objective norm of truth--Church teaching. Church teaching is clear on the issues mentioned (Cf. Catechism of the Catholic Church #1783). The theological position to the contrary is untenable and has been frequently condemned by the Magisterium of the Catholic Church. The Second Vatican Council mentioned conscience more than seventy times, never without a modifying term: "well-formed conscience, mal-formed conscience; you must form your conscience, etc."

Conscience is not to be construed as one's mere ideas and opinions, or whatever vagrant and morally vacuous thoughts race through one's mind. "Conscience is a judgment of reason whereby the human person recognizes the moral quality of a concrete act that he is going to perform, is in the process of performing, or has already completed" (Catechism of the Catholic Church #1778). It must be grounded in truth, formed to truth. For Catholics that is Church teaching in faith and morals.

Any candidate for political office, Catholic or otherwise, who is in favor of intrinsically evil things (abortion, euthanasia, same-sex marriage, etc), votes for them, or otherwise funds or furthers their cause, cannot be supported in any way by a Catholic who wishes to remain Catholic in fact, not just in name.

Catholic office holders, whether presidents, senators, congress men or women, or judges at any level must adhere to Catholic teaching or run the risk of separating themselves from the Body of Christ. In such egregious and chronic cases of gross moral evil such as instituting and perpetuating abortion and the structures of sin that surround it, it is quite probable that such Catholic officials are excommunicated in virtue of the acts themselves. A latae sententiae (automatic) excommunication is likely triggered when they vote for laws, funding, and structures that enable and perpetuate such obvious and egregious evil (Cf. Code of Canon Law, Canons 1364,1398; Canon 1329, par. #2). They are in turn forbidden from approaching the sacraments as the result (Cf. Catechism of Catholic Church #1463).

These persons must undoubtedly think that a fetus is not a human being. If they did, would they authorize and enable the wholesale and on demand execution of tens of millions of the most innocent human beings in their mothers' wombs? If they think there is not a human being in the womb, then they do not believe what the Church believes, and that belief is not optional. Such a rejection of so fundamental a truth is tantamount to heresy (Cf. Catechism of the Catholic Church #2089), the automatic penalty for which is excommunication (Cf Code of Canon Law #1364). No further act of a bishop is required either, since the act of unbelief in itself is what triggers the severing of the member from the Body. If, on the contrary, they think that indeed there is a human being in the womb, they are in a worse position, having knowingly and willingly fostered, facilitated, and perpetuated a human holocaust of unthinkable proportions.

The lame argument that they personally oppose such things as abortion, yet vote for them repeatedly, demonstrates the most virulent form of moral and political schizophrenia yet to afflict mankind. That they succeed in duping millions of otherwise intelligent people with this absurd and twisted logic does not bode well for the future of the nation that votes for them.

The further up the hierarchy of authority one goes, the more responsible and the more culpable one becomes. Hence, a supreme court justice, senator, or president who supports abortion through voting or rhetoric is significantly more culpable than a woman who effectively procures an abortion. She is responsible for one abortion; they are accomplices in millions. If she has knowledge of the seriousness of the act and the canonical penalty attached thereto, she can incur an automatic excommunication. What of those who enabled millions of such abortions? Is it to be believed that they are immune from culpability? Infinitely more deserving of the canonical penalty are those Catholic politicians who foster the laws and structures that enable such outrageous crimes against humanity.

A pastor who permits such an elected or appointed official--especially if they purport to be Catholic--to skate along relatively unscathed on such morally thin ice, is perhaps the most negligent and the most culpable of all. To fail to publicly censure such public officials is tantamount to participating in their crimes.

If there is ignorance, instruct the ignorant. If there is obstinacy, exact the canonical penalty. To fail to do so results not only in ignorance and obstinacy, but negligence and permissiveness: the fertile soil in which a degenerating culture can multiply its errors, bear evil fruit, and die. Religious leaders are in a unique position to influence the nation and the world for the better by calling their people to high moral standards. Failure to do so ultimately results in disaster, for the moral demise of a nation always precedes the ultimate demise of a nation.

Among some Church leaders there is an understandable fear of acting decisively, now. This is, obviously, because the pain of the recent sex abuse scandals is so fresh in the mind of a rightfully indignant public. However, if the Church should fail to exercise her solemn pastoral duty at such a critical moment in history, it is likely that this further lack of decisive action will prove fatal for the last vestiges of respect remaining for the leadership of the Church. Because we at times may have failed to act appropriately and decisively in one matter shouldn't consign us to a perpetual paralysis of the will to do good in other matters. Fear of criticism, loss of a tax advantage, or political expediency should never deter us from our sacred duty.

There is no excuse whatever for a Catholic politician who supports such morally outrageous perversions of authentic justice such as abortion, partial-birth abortion, euthanasia, human cloning, and same-sex marriage. The hierarchy of the Church ultimately must severely censure them and make such censure public. The sin is egregious and public. The redress must be commensurately severe and public, precisely because of that.

The hour is late indeed. Can it be imagined that the hand of the heavenly Father "who chastises every son He loves" (Cf. Jdt 8:27, Prv 3:12, Sir 30:1) will be held back indefinitely? We are poised on the edge of a precipice; a definitive moment in history has come. If the morally toxic wasteland that used to be the greatest nation on the face of the earth isn't accorded "moral super-fund" status soon, then will not the wake-up call that was 911 pale into insignificance at the moral day of reckoning that is inexorably coming? Even if one doesn't care to believe that God punishes, He surely corrects out of love, and often He uses the blunt instrument of our enemies to do so.

Every person of good will, above all Catholics in virtue of what their faith requires of them, must properly form their conscience to the objective norm of the true and the good: to that which is in accord with right reason, justice, and traditional moral values, and then vote in accordance with that well formed conscience.

God bless America!

Chapter Two
Divine Revelation

The Good News of salvation is that God our Father has revealed himself to the created universe in the person of his only son, the Lord Jesus Christ. The mysterious and transcendent God of past ages, the one who dwells in unapproachable light, made himself known to mankind's first parents in the garden. Then, through the covenant with Noah, the election of Abraham, the formation of his people Israel, the Mosaic Law, and the prophets He became more and more immanent.

As the Letter to the Hebrews tells us, in times past, God spoke in fragmentary and varied ways to our fathers through the prophets; in this the final age, he has spoken to us through his son, whom he has made heir of all things and through whom he first created the universe. This son is the reflection of the Father's glory, the exact representation of the Father's being, and he sustains all things by his powerful word (Letter to the Hebrews 1:1-3).

Jesus Christ is the eternal Word through which this revelation has been transmitted to us by the heavenly Father in the power of the Holy Spirit. Jesus Christ is the mediator and fullness of all revelation (Vatican II, Dogmatic Constitution on Divine Revelation, #2). If we would take all of the words of Scripture, all of the words of the Catechism and other important church documents, these many words all compress, condense, synthesize and distill into one word--the eternal Word--Jesus Christ. The great Carmelite saint and doctor of the church, St. John of the Cross, said it beautifully: "In giving us his Son, his only Word (for he possesses no other), he spoke everything to us at once in this sole Word--and he has no more to say...because what he spoke before to the prophets in parts, he has now spoken all at once by giving us the All Who is His Son" (Catechism #65; cf. St. John of the Cross, The Ascent of Mt. Carmel, 2, 22, 3-5). Divine revelation, quite simply, is God revealing himself to us in the person of his son, Jesus Christ. There will be no further public revelation, as the Catechism tells us (#66).

Analogies are useful, even though they are imperfect. God is one. He is also three. The one God, who is Father, Son, and Holy Spirit, has revealed himself to us. This one-only divine revelation (the Word) is transmitted to us in a written form (sacred Scripture) and an oral form (sacred Tradition), and has one-only authentic and authoritative interpreter--the magisterium of the church.

The Second Vatican Council taught very clearly and beautifully that "It is clear, therefore, that, in the supremely wise arrangement of God, sacred Tradition, sacred Scripture and the Magisterium of the Church are so connected and associated that one of them cannot subsist (stand) without the others. Working together, each in its own way under the action of the one Holy Spirit, they all contribute effectively to the salvation of souls (Dogmatic Constitution on Divine Revelation, #10).

The Lord Jesus, while on this earth, taught orally. The ones that he taught first were the 12 men that he called to be his closest collaborators in his mission of salvation, the apostles. The apostles then handed on faithfully to their successors, the bishops, what they had been taught by Christ: In order that the full and living Gospel might always be preserved in the Church the apostles left bishops as their successors. They gave them their own position of teaching authority (Dogmatic Constitution on Divine Revelation, #7). Indeed, the apostolic preaching, which is expressed in a special way in the inspired books, was to be preserved in a continuous line of succession until the end of time (Dogmatic Constitution on Divine Revelation, #8).

This living transmission, accomplished in the Holy Spirit, is called Tradition, since it is distinct from sacred Scripture, though closely connected to it. Through Tradition, the church, in her doctrine, life, and worship perpetuates and transmits to every generation all that she herself is, all that she believes (Dogmatic Constitution on Divine Revelation, #8).

So, the one-only Word of God (Jesus) is transmitted to us in an oral form (Sacred Tradition), and a written form (Sacred Scripture); and the one-only authentic and authoritative interpreter of this one-only Word of God is the church's teaching office--the magisterium. The magisterium, quite simply, is the successor of St. Peter, the bishop of Rome, the pope, and the bishops united to him. The magisterium has received a sacred deposit--the Word of God. It is not superior to the Word of God, but is its servant (#86). The magisterium faithfully hands on what it has received from Christ through the apostles--this holy word who is Christ himself.

Mindful of Christ's words to his apostles--"He who hears you, hears me" (Luke 10:16)--the faithful receive the teachings and directives that their pastors give them in different forms. There is an erroneous and dangerous notion in some church circles today that all that the faithful have to accept from the magisterium are ex cathedra dogmatic definitions from the pope. This is absolutely false. As Vatican II and the Catechism clearly assert, the faithful receive with docility the teachings and directives that their pastors give them in different forms (Vatican II, Lumen Gentium, #20).

Encyclicals, apostolic letters and exhortations, post-synodal apostolic exhortations, the Code of Canon Law, and the other manifestations of ordinary magisterium are to be accepted with docility and the full religious assent of mind and will by all the faithful. Theologians, religious educators, and other private persons constitute no parallel magisterium. They can provide advice and insights to the bishops and the Holy Father, but they have no authority whatever to deviate from the teaching of the magisterium.

There is no such thing as legitimate dissent from authentic and authoritative magisterial teaching. The word more properly is not dissent, but disobedience. The words that conclude the passage from the Gospel of Luke cited from Vatican II above are relevant: "He who hears you, hears me. He who rejects you, rejects me. And he who rejects me, rejects him who sent me" (Luke 10:16).

God our loving Father has revealed himself to

us, giving us the unimaginably generous gift of his Word. This Word is transmitted to us in the form of Sacred Tradition, Sacred Scripture, and magisterial teaching, no one of which can stand without the other two. May we be thankful for, and ever-faithful to this gift.

Through all the words of Sacred Scripture, God speaks only one single Word, his one Utterance in whom he expresses himself completely (CCC 102; cf. Heb 1:1-3). Jesus Christ, the eternal Word, is what every word found in Sacred Scripture is ultimately about.

God himself is the author of Sacred Scripture (CCC 105), and because of that the Word of God as transmitted to us in the Bible is to be accepted as inspired and true. We accept it, as we do the Doctrine of the Faith in general, not because it sounds plausible to us, but because of the One who has given it to us--God, who is Truth itself; the One who can neither deceive nor be deceived (VATICAN I, Dei Filius, 3, Denzinger Schînmetzer 3008).

God, the Author of Sacred Scripture, transmitted his Word to us by inspiring the human authors of Scripture (CCC 106; cf. VATICAN II, Dei Verbum 11). The Catechism asserts what Vatican II asserted, which is what the Church has always asserted: that Sacred Scripture teaches the truth. We are obliged to accept as true all that the inspired authors affirm, for through them it is the Holy Spirit who is affirming this truth, thus, We must acknowledge that the books of Sacred Scripture firmly, faithfully, and without error teach that truth which God, for the sake of our salvation, wished to see confided to the Sacred Scriptures (CCC 107; cf. VATICAN II, Dei

Verbum 11).

As is the case when trying to understand and properly construe anything transmitted by language--whether written or spoken--certain principles have to be followed. Through Sacred Scripture God in his great love for us speaks to us in a human way. Therefore, in order to interpret Scripture correctly the reader must be attentive to trying to understand what the human authors were really trying to say. It is the Church, our holy Mother and Teacher, who shows us how to do this. We are to pay attention to such things as the language, culture, modes of feeling and narrating current at the time of the human authors writing (Cf. CCC 109-110).

But, since Sacred Scripture is inspired, there is another and no less important principle of correct interpretation, without which Scripture would remain a dead letter. "Sacred Scripture must be read and interpreted in the light of the same Spirit by whom it was written"(CCC 111; cf. Dei Verbum 12). The greatest gifts of intellect, expertise in biblical languages, etc., although of great value, account for nothing ultimately if the person is not filled with the same Holy Spirit who inspired Sacred Scripture in the first place.

The acid test of whether or not a person in fact is operating in the Holy Spirit is humility. If one is humble one has the desire and the true freedom of will to obey legitimate Church authority. One who does not have this essential virtue of humility will ultimately rebel against the authentic and authoritative teaching of the Magisterium of the Church--the only legitimate interpreter ultimately of God's Word, whether written or passed on in the oral form of Sacred Tradition.

The Catechism (#113) reminds us of the three criteria which the Second Vatican Council (Dei Verbum 12) lays down for us to insure that we interpret Sacred Scripture in accordance with the same Spirit who inspired it in the first place:

1) Be especially attentive "to the content and unity of the whole of Scripture."

2) Read the Scripture within "the living Tradition of the whole Church." According to a saying of the Fathers, Sacred Scripture is written principally in the Church's heart rather than in documents and records, for the Church carries in her Tradition the living memorial of God's Word, and it is the Holy Spirit who gives her the spiritual interpretation of the Scripture.

3) Be attentive to the analogy of faith (Cf. Rom 12:6). By analogy of faith we mean the coherence of the truths of faith among themselves and within the whole plan of Revelation.

The very commendable growth in interest in the study of Sacred Scripture which often manifests itself in Bible study groups must take the teaching of Vatican II into account. These three principles must be used in order to insure that what we are really doing is interpreting the written Word of God in accordance with the Spirit who inspired it in the first place.

On a practical note, I highly recommend The Navarre Bible, a unique set of commentaries on the New Testament books published by Four Courts Press and distributed in the United States by Scepter Press. It is available from most good Catholic book stores, as well as direct from Scepter Press. This set, prepared by the

Ecclesiastical Faculty of Theology of the University of Navarre, beautifully incorporates all of the principles above stated in a very simple, readable, and spiritually enriching presentation. It can be a great help to Scripture study groups or to individuals who desire to read the Bible as the Catholic Church does.

As we know, the Bible did not somehow merely drop out of the sky; it came to us through the Church. It was by the apostolic Tradition that the Church through her Magisterium discerned which writings were inspired and should be included in what we call the Canon of Sacred Scripture. There are 46 books that comprise the Old Testament and 27 the New Testament. Sacred Tradition and the Magisterium of the Church set before us what we today call the Bible (CCC 120).

The Old and New Testaments constitute one-only written Word of God. The New Testament did not revoke the Old Covenant (CCC 121). The Old Testament is the true Word of God and sheds light on the New, prefiguring and preparing for the full manifestation of the eternal Word spoken of in the New Testament--Jesus, the Christ. It is only in the full light of the New Testament that we can properly understand the Old Testament. Hence, the New Testament did not do away with the Ten Commandments of the Mosaic Law, the admonitions of the prophets, or the wisdom and counsel of the Wisdom Books; it fulfilled and consummated them.

The Gospels are the heart of all the Scriptures "because they are our principal source for the life and teaching of the Incarnate Word, our Savior (CCC 125; Dei Verbum 18). The Catechism, as always, adhering to the teaching of the Second Vatican Council, distinguishes three stages in the formation of the Gospels (CCC 126; cf. Dei Verbum 19):

1) The life and teaching of Jesus. The Church holds firmly that the four Gospels, whose historicity she unhesitatingly affirms, faithfully hand on what Jesus, the Son of God, while he lived among men, really did and taught for their eternal salvation, until the day when he was taken up.

2) The oral tradition. For, after the ascension of the Lord, the apostles handed on to their hearers what he had said and done, but with that fuller understanding which they, instructed by the glorious events of Christ and enlightened by the Spirit of Truth, now enjoyed.

3) The written Gospels. The sacred authors, in writing the four Gospels, selected certain of the many elements which had been handed on, either orally or already in written form; others they synthesized or explained with an eye to the situation of the churches, while sustaining the form of preaching, but always in such a fashion that they have told us the honest truth about Jesus.

The Sacred Scriptures, quite simply, tell us the honest truth about Jesus--the eternal Word. Hence, our good and holy Mother, the Catholic Church, forcefully and specifically exhorts all the Christian faithful...to learn "the surpassing knowledge of Jesus Christ" by frequent reading of the divine Scriptures. Ignorance of the Scriptures is ignorance of Christ" (CCC 133; cf. Dei Verbum 25).

Chapter Three
Upon This Rock,
I Shall Build My Church

Reflecting the thought of the church through the ages, the Catechism (#760) reminds us that Christians of the first centuries said, "The world was created for the sake of the Church." God created the world for the sake of communion with his divine life, a communion brought about by the "convocation" of men in Christ, and this "convocation" is the Church. Many people have problems with the Church quite simply because they do not understand its origins, its mission, or its end. The Catholic Church is not a mere human invention, like a political or social entity. The Church is of divine institution; Jesus Christ himself instituted the Church, not mere men after his Ascension (#763-766).

We recall a striking scene from the Gospel of Matthew: Jesus and his disciples are passing through the region of Caesarea Philippi--a region known for its pagan religions. The Master asks his disciples who they say that the Son of Man is. It was perhaps one of the first public opinion polls regarding Christianity. The results of such polls of mere personal opinions, then as now, are less than satisfying: "Some say John the Baptizer, others Elijah, still others Jeremiah or one of the prophets." These were conflicting and contradictory guesses and opinions that have none of the ring of authority and authenticity the human spirit needs in order to walk confidently in the dark night of faith. Then, one voice rang out, the voice of Simon: "You are the Messiah, the Son of the living God!" The response of the Lord is the definitive answer when it comes to answering the question, "Who founded the Church?": "Blest are you, Simon son of John! No mere man has revealed this to you, but my heavenly Father. I for my part declare to you, you are 'Rock,' and on this rock I will build my church, and the jaws of death shall not prevail against it." Note who the "I" is: the "I" is a divine person, the subject of action is divine; God himself institutes the Church. The Church is not a mere human institution. Christ, the eternal Word, the Father's Son, institutes and builds his Church on the "Rock."

All through the Old Testament, "Rock" with an uppercase "R" refers to God himself Then in the Gospel of Matthew referred to above, we see Jesus, the "Rock," because he is a divine subject of action, renaming Simon "Rock." Jesus, the real "Rock," is also referred to as the "bridegroom" or "groom" as well in Scripture. The Church is his "bride" (#796). We know, also from the Word, that in marriage, whether natural or supernatural, the "two become one flesh." Jesus and his church are one; bridegroom and bride are one. Hence, Christ is naming Peter "Rock", one with himself. There is no other "Rock" other than Christ absolutely speaking. However, the Rock, in a mystical marriage, unites his beloved bride, the Church, to himself. Simon is named "Rock", and whoever hears the Rock Peter is hearing the Rock who is Christ; whoever rejects the Rock who is Peter, rejects the Rock Christ and the One who sent him, the Father.

You cannot separate the Lord Jesus from his

beloved body and bride, the Church. To reject the teaching of Peter and his successors the Roman pontiffs, together with the bishops who are united with the Holy Father in teaching the one faith which has been handed down faithfully form the apostles, is to reject the teaching of Jesus Christ, and the One who sent him, the Father (cf. Luke 10:16).

The Catholic Church can never fail ultimately, although her members can and do. The Church is far more than the sum of her human members, for if that were the case the Church would surely have fallen long ago. The most important member of the Church is her head, Christ the Lord (#792-795). The soul of the Church, the life-giving power, the animator and sanctifier of the Church, is the Holy Spirit. The head and soul of the Church is God; the Church will never fail. The storms of time and the tempests stirred up by earthly kings and rulers come and go; their crowns rise, and fall, and roll in the dust, but the Church goes on. Mere personal opinions come and go. Some say this, some say that, but mere personal opinion cannot move the Rock.

Head and body are one; bridegroom and bride are one. Those who attack the Church attack Christ. When Saul of Tarsus was persecuting the newborn church on his way to Damascus, he was knocked off his horse by the light who is Christ. "He fell to the ground and at the same time heard a voice saying, 'Saul, Saul, why do you persecute me?' 'Who are you, sir?' he asked. The voice answered, 'I am Jesus, the one you are persecuting.'" Saul was "breathing murderous threats against the Lord's disciples," against the Church.

Christ told him clearly that he was persecuting him, Jesus, the Lord. Christ and his church are one. To love Jesus truly, we must love his church.

In an age of violence and violent change, it is comforting to know that we are so intimately one with Christ, residing in his body, as his body and his bride, the Church. Transcending time and space, the Church is relevant to all people at all times and in all places. Indeed, to be rooted in the Rock, to be one with the Rock, keeps us from being swept away by the strife and storms of any time and any place.

Chapter Four
The Church is One

On Sundays and solemnities the Church professes the Nicene Creed. Part of our profession of faith concerns the Church; and as the Catechism (#811) teaches: "This is the sole Church of Christ, which in the Creed we profess to be one, holy, catholic and apostolic." These four characteristics, inseparably linked with each other, indicate essential features of the Church and her mission. The Church does not possess them of herself; it is Christ who, through the Holy Spirit, makes his Church one, holy, catholic, and apostolic, and it is he who calls her to realize each of these qualities.

The Church is one because of her source, the blessed Trinity--the unity of the Trinity of Persons of one God: the Father, Son, and Holy Spirit (#813; Cf. Vatican II, Unitatis redintegratio, 5).

The Church is one also because of her founder, the one Lord and savior, the only Son of God, the only name by which a man can be saved: Jesus the Christ (#813).

Likewise, the Church is one because of her soul, the form of the body of Christ, the life-giving principle: the Holy Spirit. The Holy Spirit brings about that unity which is of the very essence of the Church (#813). Although the Church is one and one only, there is a legitimate diversity within this one church. This is due to the variety of God's gifts and the great diversity of those who receive these gifts (#814). The many peoples, cultures, rites, and ways of prayer, rather than eroding unity, demonstrate the dynamic richness of the Church's oneness. The reality of sin, however, is always at work, and the unity that God intended for his Church is constantly threatened.

There are certain bonds of unity which hold the fabric of the Church together. First of all, as St. Paul teaches, there is charity, "which binds everything together in perfect harmony" (Col 3:14). In addition, the Catechism lists three visible bonds of communion which insure unity, if they are observed and maintained:

1. Profession of one faith which is received from the Apostles. Jesus Christ taught his Apostles the truth, which is God himself in essence. They then handed on this essential teaching in faith and morals to their successors: the bishops in union with the visible head of the Church, the successor of St. Peter, the pope. Remaining absolutely and uncompromisingly faithful to this one faith preserves the unity of the Church. Stepping outside of this one faith, rejecting any single tenet of this one faith sets in motion the forces of disunity--which is nothing less than a death wish, for the very principle of death is disunity. As things begin to break down, working out of harmony with each other, the life-giving forces of integrity fail and death holds sway.

2. Common celebration of divine worship, especially of the sacraments. The Church herself establishes her liturgical norms and rubrics, and although the legitimate differences in the various rites within the Catholic Church manifest the richness of her unity, the integrity of these rites

themselves has to be maintained. Only the Church herself can establish her liturgical norms and rubrics. No individual has any authority to make essential changes in what the Church has laid down as her normative practice, whether in liturgy, doctrine or law. One should be able to just as easily recognize the celebration of the Eucharist in Peoria as Paris.

3. Apostolic succession through the sacrament of holy orders, maintaining the fraternal concord of God's family. Christ, the head of his Church, instituted his Church on the confession of faith of Peter. He grafted Simon the son of John into himself, making him one with the Rock--Christ himself; and, hence, he named him "Rock" or Peter. The sacrament of holy orders is of the essence for the Church. There can be no authentic church whatever without the successors of the Apostles; those who are ordained for their ministry through the sacrament of holy orders.

As the Catechism (#816) clearly teaches: "The sole Church of Christ [is that] which our Savior, after his Resurrection, entrusted to Peter's pastoral care, commissioning him and the other apostles to extend and rule it....This Church, constituted and organized as a society in the present world, subsists in the Catholic Church, which is governed by the successor of Peter and by the bishops in communion with him" (Vatican II, Lumen gentium, 8, 2).

The Second Vatican Council's Decree on Ecumenism explains: "For it is through Christ's Catholic Church alone, which is the universal help toward salvation, that the fullness of the means of salvation can be obtained. It was to the apostolic college alone, of which Peter is the head, that we believe that our Lord entrusted all the blessings of the New Covenant, in order to establish on earth the one Body of Christ into which all those should be fully incorporated who belong in any way to the People of God" (Vatican II, Unitatis redintegratio, 3, 5).

As we know, there have been wounds to this unity desired by Christ from the very beginning. Often enough, as the Church has taught, "men of both sides were to blame" (#817). In our time we cannot charge with the sin of heresy, apostasy, or schism those who are born into the various communities we have come to call "Protestant." The Catholic Church accepts our Protestant brothers and sisters with respect and affection (#818). As the Catechism reminds us, "All who have been justified by faith in Baptism are incorporated into Christ; they therefore have a right to be called Christians, and with good reason are accepted as brothers in the Lord by the children of the Catholic Church" (#818).

As true children of our heavenly Father we must long for and work towards that day when indeed there will be "one shepherd and one flock." The Church teaches us some very concrete ways by which we can work towards this much desired unity (#821). The first two constitute the heart of authentic ecumenism, and the only way the cause of unity will ever truly be furthered:

1. "A permanent renewal of the Church in greater fidelity to her vocation." When we Catholics begin to live what we profess with intensity then others will be attracted to the Catholic Church. Spiritual tepidity, a mere

"going through the motions" will never attract others to the Church. The word "lukewarm" is used once in all of Scripture. In the book of Revelation "The Amen", Jesus, in his message to the Church at Latakia says, "I know your deeds; I know you are neither hot nor cold. How I wish you were one or the other--hot or cold! But because you are lukewarm, neither hot nor cold, I will spew you out of my mouth!"

2. "Conversion of heart as the faithful try to live holier lives according to the Gospel." The only way the Church will be all that she is called to be is by individual members of the Church becoming truly holy. Personal holiness is the answer and the only answer to all of the Church's problems, and the world's.

Great is the mystery of our faith, and great is both the mystery and the gift of the one church of Jesus Christ. May we pray constantly and work actively that indeed the longing of Christ's own heart may be fulfilled: that there might be once again one shepherd and one flock.

Chapter Five
The Church is Holy

At a time in the church's history when scandal and infidelity shake, if not destroy the faith of many, we recall that the church is "unfailingly holy." As the Catechism reminds us (#823), "The Church...is held, as a matter of faith, to be unfailingly holy. This is because Christ, the Son of God, who with the Father and the Spirit is hailed as 'alone holy,' loved the Church as his Bride, giving himself up for her so as to sanctify her; he joined her to himself as his body and endowed her with the gift of the Holy Spirit for the glory of God" (Vatican II, Lumen Gentium, 12).

If we entertain the mistaken notion that the church is merely the sum of her human members, then we run the risk of eventually trying to reject such an imperfect organism. There is a spiritual principle that many of us would do well to remember: Focus on the light, not on the darkness. If we continually seek the flaws and imperfections in the members of the body of Christ, the church, surely we shall find them. Focus on the darkness and you run the very real risk of being absorbed into the darkness, of becoming part of the darkness. Focus on the light and you will be absorbed in the light and indeed become light to the world in the one who is the "Light of the world."

So often we become discouraged because some individual through human weakness wounds the body of Christ. The person may be a priest or religious, and we take offense because of the weakness of those we look up to. We may ourselves be much worse than the one who the media criticizes due to some sin or scandal, for perhaps we have been given more by God and responded less than the poor person in the scandal spotlight this week.

The fact of the matter is that only God has a seat high enough to see everything in order to arrive at a just and valid judgment about a person's guilt or innocence and the degree thereof. It just doesn't pay to rashly judge any individual, although we must make rational judgments in the objective order. Attempting to judge individuals and subjectively impute guilt to them results in the loss of interior peace, and we begin to think that the church is less than good, less than holy; perhaps even that the body of Christ is evil.

The church is holy because of her head who is personified holiness; because of her soul: the Holy Spirit, and because of those imperfect and weak human beings who through grace become one with Christ through the action of the Holy Spirit. Indeed, the church is the "'holy People of God' and her members are called 'saints'" (#823). To the degree that we, through humility, obedience and docility, allow the Holy Spirit to form Christ within us, we become an active force to make the holiness of the church present to a world much in need of such holiness.

Indeed, united with Christ, the church is sanctified by him; through him and with him she becomes sanctifying. "All the activities of the Church are directed, as towards their end, to the sanctification of men in Christ and the glorification of God" (Vatican II, Sacrosanctum Concilium, 10). It is in the church that the "fullness of the means of salvation" (Vatican II, Unitatis redintegratio, 3, 5) has been deposited. It is in her that "by the grace of God we acquire holiness" (#824; Cf. Vatican II, Lumen Gentium, 48).

Regardless of the deficiencies and sins of individual members of the church we should have a great love for, and gratitude to, this unfailingly holy body and bride of Jesus Christ. It is through Christ's body the church that we are reborn in baptism; that we are strengthened in the faith through confirmation; that we are united so intimately with Jesus, the church's head through Eucharist; that we are raised from spiritual death to life by having our sins forgiven through the sacrament of penance; that man and woman become sacramentally "one flesh" in the "Word who became flesh and dwelt among us" in the sacrament of matrimony;" that we receive a ministerial priesthood capacitated to give us five of the seven sacraments through holy orders; and it is through the church that we are strengthened in suffering, often for the final journey to eternity, in the sacrament of anointing of the sick. The indefectibly holy church bestows holy things upon God's holy people, making them holy.

As the Catechism, echoing the Second Vatican Council, teaches us, "The Church on earth is endowed already with a sanctity that is real though imperfect" (#825; Cf. Vatican II, Lumen Gentium, 48, 3). We are called to make use of the many means of salvation which the church holds out to us in order to actualize our potential for that holiness that we are called to in Christ. We are all sinners, and we must acknowledge that often more than obvious fact. All of us are sinners: priests, religious, lay faithful; all of us without exception. Only Jesus and his holy mother are without sin. That being the case we should be slow to judge, quick to understand, quicker to forgive those who do fall, especially those who fall from high places.

No one knows how much pressure and pain are brought to bear by the forces of evil against the shepherds of the sheep. The church's holy ones, the saints, were the first to acknowledge that "except for the grace of God, there go I." None of us on this earth has yet arrived at our destination; we are work in process, on the way but not home yet.

No matter how weak and deficient we may feel, we should not use this weakness, however, as an excuse for sloth. We are called to holiness of life in Christ through the power of his Spirit. In fact, we must "be holy (perfected) as our Father in heaven is perfect." It is a divine mandate, not a mere suggestion! Holiness is the hidden source of the church's apostolic activity and missionary zeal (#828).

We know that God is perfectly faithful in accordance with his very nature. He has called us in the church to holiness and he has given us the full means of salvation through his holy church. It is comforting to know that one of us, "Our tainted nature's solitary boast," the Blessed Virgin Mary, is the perfect fulfillment of the church's destiny. Mary, without sin, reigns with her Son forever. She is "our life, our sweetness, and our hope" as mother of the church. We acknowledge our sinfulness, but with great and unfailing hope we look to our spiritual mother, for, as the Catechism (#829) reminds us, "... in the most Blessed Virgin the Church has already reached that perfection whereby she exists without spot or wrinkle, the faithful still strive to conquer sin and increase in holiness. And so they turn their eyes to Mary" (Cf. Vatican II, Lumen Gentium, 65); in her, the church is already the "all holy."

Chapter Six
The Church is Catholic

We have used the term 'Catholic' so many times in our lives that we tend to take it for granted. Since words are of the utmost importance, it seems necessary to look more carefully at this very important word in our vocabulary.

It is generally acknowledged that the word Catholic Church first appears in the writings of the apostolic father, St. Ignatius of Antioch, in his Letter To the Smyrnaeans in the year 110 A.D. The context of the use of the term is as follows: Wherever the bishop appears, let the people be there; just as wherever Jesus Christ is, there is the Catholic Church. As the Catechism of the Catholic Church (#830) states: The word catholic means universal, in the sense of according to the totality or in keeping with the whole. The Church is catholic in a double sense: First, the Church is catholic because Christ is present in her. Where there is Christ Jesus, there is the Catholic Church (St. Ignatius). In her subsists the fullness of Christ's body united with its head; this implies that she receives from him the fullness of the means of salvation which he has willed: correct and complete confession of faith, full sacramental life, and ordained ministry in apostolic succession. The Church was, in this fundamental sense, catholic on the day of Pentecost and will always be so until the day of the Parousia.

Secondly, the Church is catholic (#831) because she has been sent out by Christ on a mission to the whole of the human race. Wherever the faithful gather united under their pastors the universal Church is made present. Hence, in Sacramento the universal or "Catholic" Church gathers and celebrates, teaches and serves. As the Catechism (#834) states: Particular Churches [i.e., dioceses] are fully catholic through their communion with one of them, the Church of Rome which presides in charity. For with this church, by reason of its pre-eminence, the whole Church, that is the faithful everywhere, must necessarily be in accord. Indeed, from the incarnate Word's descent to us, all Christian churches everywhere have held and hold the great Church that is here [at Rome] to be their only basis and foundation since, according to the Savior's promise, the gates of hell have never prevailed against her. It is through union with Rome--obedience to the bishop of Rome, the pope--that full incorporation into the church that Christ instituted upon "Peter" is guaranteed. The Holy Father is the guarantor of unity, and it is through faithful obedience and union with his office and his teaching that the church's unity, holiness, catholicity, and apostolicity are guaranteed.

The Catechism clarifies the question of who belongs to the Catholic Church: "All men are called to this catholic unity of the People of God....And to it, in different ways, belong or are ordered: the Catholic faithful, others who believe in Christ, and finally all mankind, called by God's grace to salvation" (#836). There are certain criteria which determine full incorporation into the one church instituted by Jesus Christ: those, who possessing the Spirit of

Christ, accept all the means of salvation given to the church together with her entire organization; and who by the bonds constituted by the profession of faith, the sacraments, ecclesiastical government, and communion--are joined in the visible structure of the Church of Christ who rules her through the Supreme Pontiff and the bishops (#837).

However, it is to be soberly remembered that simply being a member of the Catholic Church is no guarantee of salvation. "When much has been given a man, much will be required of him. More will be asked of a man to whom more has been entrusted" (Luke 12:48b). In the Catholic Church we have all seven of the sacraments, and we have been given the fullness of divine Revelation, since we have not only Scripture tradition as well; and the church's magisterium, which is necessary to authentically and authoritatively interpret the Word of God, whether written in the Bible or handed down by the apostolic tradition. Catholics are thus required to live a life much more in accord with the Spirit of Christ. The gift is great, but so too is the responsibility.

The church has a real relationship with all mankind, for all are called to the perfection of charity, and that can be achieved only by using the full means the Lord has given us. All Christians, Jews, Muslims, and the entire human race are our brothers and sisters, and they are called to the fullness of the church's blessings. It would be a false ecumenism which did not desire ardently that all men would enter into the fullness of Catholic unity in the church instituted by Jesus the Christ.

All salvation comes from Jesus Christ, the

head of his mystical body, through his body, the church. Hence, there is indeed no salvation outside the church. The Second Vatican Council teaches clearly that the church is necessary for salvation: Jesus himself explicitly asserted the necessity of faith and Baptism, and thereby affirmed at the same time the necessity of the Church which men enter through Baptism as through a door. Hence they could not be saved who, knowing that the Catholic Church was founded as necessary by God through Christ, would refuse either to enter it or to remain in it (Vatican II, Lumen gentium, 14; Catechism #846). The Catechism makes it clear, however, that this affirmation is not aimed at those who, through no fault of their own, do not know Christ and his church (#847). "Although in ways known to himself God can lead those who, through no fault of their own, are ignorant of the Gospel, to that faith without which it is impossible to please him, the Church still has the obligation and also the sacred right to evangelize all men" (Vatican II, Ad gentes, 7; Catechism #848). We know that God can use extraordinary means to save any person, but the only ordinary means of salvation we know of is through the church, the "universal sacrament of salvation."

Hence, missionary activity is an absolute requirement of the church's catholicity: Having been divinely sent to the nations that she might be the universal sacrament of salvation, the church, in obedience to the command of her founder and because it is demanded by her own essential universality, strives to preach the Gospel to all men" (Vatican II, Ad gentes, 1; Catechism #849). Having "put on the mind of

Christ," being filled with the Holy Spirit, the protagonist and principal agent of the whole of the Church's mission, each and every one of us in the Catholic Church should long for the day when there is "one Shepherd and one flock." We should desire most sincerely that all persons have what we have: the full means of salvation-- all seven sacraments, celebrated licitly and validly, as well as the fullness of divine Revelation. How can we be content until every one of our brothers and sisters believe what we believe and have Jesus himself in the Eucharist, which is the source, the center, and the summit of Christian life? May the God who is One grant us this gift of his universal love for humankind!

Chapter Seven
The Church is Apostolic

As the Catechism of the Catholic Church teaches us, the church is apostolic because she is founded on the apostles in three ways. "She was and remains built on the foundation of the apostles, the witnesses chosen and sent on mission by Christ himself; with the help of the Spirit dwelling in her, the church keeps and hands on the teaching, the 'good deposit,' the salutary words she has heard from the apostles; she continues to be taught, sanctified, and guided by the apostles until Christ's return, through their successors in pastoral office: the college of bishops, assisted by priests, in union with the successor of Peter, the church's supreme pastor." (#857).

Jesus Christ taught his apostles in a very direct and intimate way, and they in turn were to hand on his teaching faithfully to the entire world. The bishops in union with the successor of St. Peter, the pope, continue to hand on faithfully what Christ taught. This is a "sacred deposit." It is the "doctrine of the faith." This is something received, not made up as we go along. It is for the Holy Father and the bishops who are in union with him by virtue of their apostolic office and adherence to the same teaching which they have received from those who preceded them, to authentically and authoritatively interpret this "sacred deposit of the doctrine of the faith."

The mission of the apostles and their successors is to carry on the mission of Christ the Lord. This mission is nothing other than redemption. To put it clearly and even bluntly: to save souls, to lead people to heaven, and to keep them out of hell. There are two ultimate destinies for every human: heaven or hell. (Purgatory is a final purification; all there are just passing through on their way to heaven.)

Our ultimate abode is a function of free will. "Before man are life and death, whichever he chooses shall be given him" (Sirach 15:17). God has given us an intellect which naturally tends toward truth if we do not impair and destroy its powers through serious sin. "The man who sins becomes a slave of sin," (John 8:34) the Lord Jesus said. The successors of the apostles, the bishops, are charged with the solemn responsibility of saving souls.

The church teaches that the bishops have indeed, by divine institution, taken the place of the apostles as pastors of the church, in such a way what whoever listens to them is listening to Christ, and whoever despises them despises Christ and him who sent Christ (#862; Vatican II, Lumen Gentium 20, 2). It is not a small thing to disobey, or worse, to despise a bishop or the Holy Father. All Catholic Christians must respect, obey and indeed love their bishops and the Holy Father, or they run the real risk of being held in contempt of the One who consecrated and sent these men on mission: the Lord.

It has become all too common today to criticize or condemn the Holy Father and the bishops who are united with him. Even religious and priests are seen at times on national television, or in their respective pulpits, railing against the pope or their own bishop. The faithful should pray for these persons, for they are indeed disoriented spiritually, and on the edge of a precipice. "Whoever despises them (the pope and bishops) despises Christ and him who sent Christ" (#862; Vatican II, Lumen Gentium 20, 2).

The entire church and every member of the church is apostolic. This is so because the church perdures, through the successors of St. Peter, the bishops, in communion of faith and life with her origin; and in that she is sent out into the entire world on the mission of Christ, which is redemption (#863). Every one of us as a baptized Christian must have the Master's interests in mind and at hand. We are each called to work assiduously for the building up of the Kingdom of God. This continually relates back to the mission of salvation for which the "Word became flesh and dwelt among us."

Each of us as "apostles," as persons sent on mission by the Lord through his church, must take seriously the business of being salt and light in the world. Salt not only gives savor to things, it also preserves them from spoiling. One could very easily say that the very fabric of our society, the very fabric of being, is now in danger of rotting due to an apostasy from reality and truth, from goodness and moral ways of thinking and acting. Each of us, in keeping with the apostolic nature of our lives, must be the salt of the earth that prevents the moral decay of the world around us.

Chapter Eight
The Catechism of
The Catholic Church

"Guarding the deposit of faith is the mission which the Lord entrusted to His church, and which he fulfills in every age." (John Paul II, Apostolic Constitution Fidei Depositum, On the Publication of the Catechism of the Catholic Church, prepared following the Second Vatican Council, October 11, 1992.) With these words, the Holy Father, Pope John Paul II, introduced the Catechism of the Catholic Church.

The Catechism is a direct result of the Second Vatican Council, fulfilling the principal task entrusted to that Council by Pope John XXIII: to guard and present better the precious deposit of Christian doctrine in order to make it more accessible to the Christian faithful and to all people of good will. (Pope John XXIII, Discourse at the Opening of the Second Vatican Ecumenical Council, October 11, 1962: AAS 54 (1962), pp. 788-91.) Exactly thirty years after John XXIII opened the Council (October 11, 1962) his successor, John Paul II, formally presented the Catechism of the Catholic Church to the Church and the world (October 11, 1992)--a gift of Vatican II.

First of all, let me preface what we are about to attempt in a series of articles which are apt to take as much as two years to complete. The object of our consideration is nothing less than God himself, made present in time and space in the Person of Jesus Christ, the image of the invisible God (Col. 1:15; cf. 2 Cor. 4:4) who is the Truth by his own assertion (Jn. 4;16). This quintessential truth is a divine Some-body, not a mere some-thing. This divine Teacher taught himself, not something extrinsic to himself. The teaching of Jesus Christ is the teaching of the Church, and the Catechism of the Catholic Church is a statement of the Church's faith and of catholic doctrine...a sure norm for the teaching the faith. (John Paul II, Apostolic Constitution Fidei Depositum, 3.) As stated, the Catechism is the legitimate child of the Second Vatican Council, not above the Council, but one with the Council. The Catechism of the Catholic Church articulates the Faith of the Church in a systematic and organic way, incorporating into itself the essential teaching of the Council. The most cursory reading of the Catechism shows precisely how replete with the Council's teaching (and the Church's previous Councils' teaching as well) the Catechism is.

The Catechism is, first of all, meant for bishops, for they are the principal catechists of the Church. It was felt that in the hands of the entire episcopate, the Catechism would facilitate unity. The bishops likewise can guarantee the authentic infusion of the essential contents of the Catechism into local situations. This, however, would not have been enough if only the bishops were the intended readership of the Catechism. Such a construal would not have corresponded to our renewed understanding of the Church via Vatican II. The laity are likewise responsible for the faithful transmission of the Church's faith. They are not merely passive recipients of the deposit of faith, but they also participate in its development through the sensu fidei, and they have a serious responsibility to hand on faithfully what they have received to their children. The Catechism was much needed for the individual Christian, and its sales to date close the case as to whether or not the faithful want it. Close to ten million copies are in print after a very short time! It is a best seller by all accounts.

The Catechism is a stellar example of harmonious cooperation between primacy (the Pope) and collegiality (college of bishops united to the Pope). This corresponds beautifully to both the spirit and the letter of the Second Vatican Council, as Cardinal Ratzinger expresses: ...the Catechism is de facto a collegial work; canonically, it falls under the special jurisdiction of the Pope, inasmuch as it was authorized for the whole Christian world by the Holy Father in virtue of the supreme teaching authority invested in him...The Pope is not speaking over the heads of the bishops. On the contrary, he invites his brothers in the episcopate to join him in letting the symphony of the faith ring out. He draws together the whole and secures it with his authority, which is not something imposed from without but rather something that gives the common witness its concrete, public validity. (J. Ratzinger & C. Schonborn, Introduction to the Catechism of the Catholic Church, Ignatius Press, 1994, pp. 26.)

Flowing ultimately from the Council, and immediately from the extraordinary synod of bishops of 1985, the Catechism is the result of a monumental collaboration of all the world's bishops, who received a prodigious amount of input from the ecclesiastical faculties of theology around the world, as well as numerous individual theologians and scholars. The result is truly one brought forth by the Holy Spirit through the Church universal.

What are presented in the Catechism is not one faction's personal opinions or theological hypothesizing, but the solid, objective and definitive Faith - what the Catholic Church believes and teaches authentically and authoratively. It is not a book containing merely one perspective; it is the objective and essentially immutable doctrine of faith - in short, the Truth, the teaching of Jesus Christ. It must be approached that way.

The Catechism presents the unchangeable Truth in a way that is up-to-date and relevant to precisely this age in history, remembering that the essential contents of what is presented transcends all times and all cultures, hence being limited to none and helpful to all; it being understood that the Catechism will be adapted to the languages and the cultures of today through local catechisms. What is presented by the Catechism of the Catholic Church is nothing less than Jesus Christ. He alone is both the Teacher and the Object of catechesis. This being the case, the words of the author of the Letter to the Hebrews prove helpful, "Jesus Christ is the same, yesterday, today and forever, therefore do not be carried away by all kinds of strange teaching" (Heb. 13:8-9).

In a world that often fails to discern the difference between what can change and what cannot, it is good to know that what we believe and are called to live in its essence has not and cannot change. The Truth is a Rock, and we build our house upon that Rock who is essentially Jesus

Christ, the chief Cornerstone upon which the Church is built the Truth himself. The Catechism of the Catholic Church articulates what Catholics believe and are called to live and celebrate. With our house built solidly on this Rock of Truth we can say, let the rains of confusion come, let the storms of time and culture lash against our house, we shall not be swept away, for we have built our house upon solid Rock, not upon the shifting sands of mere personal opinions nor ideas that come and go with the passing of ages.

Chapter Nine
Bring Emmanuel
To All The World

Only God could have given us a gift so unimaginable that after 2,000 years we still seem scarcely able to fathom it. The architect of all that is gave us himself. The eternal Father, who created everything through his only Word, willed that the Word become flesh and dwell among us.

Since the moment of the original sin when darkness and death entered Eden, man had labored under the heavy weight of banishment from the kingdom. The gates of heaven were closed, like the gates of the garden. Pain and death were a dark specter that haunted and frightened man, the legacy of that arrogance which inevitably results in disobedience--which just as inevitably ushers in a reign of death.

Then in the fullness of time God sent forth his Son born of a woman, born under the law, to deliver from the law those who were subjected to it, so that we might receive our status as adopted sons (Galatians 4:4-5). What a night this night of Christ's birth! As the book of Wisdom puts it, "For when peaceful stillness compassed everything and the night in its swift course was half-spent, Your all powerful Word from heaven's royal throne bounded down, a fierce warrior into the doomed land, bearing the sharp sword of your inexorable decree" (Wisdom 18:14-16).

Humble and unnoticed by the busy world, a poor couple wandered in the night, tired and cold. There was no room for them in the place where travelers lodged (Luke 2:7), fashioning a cold more intense within external cold. To his own he came, yet his own did not accept him (John 1:11). "How cruel," we say, yet "the more things change, the more they stay the same."

Today Jesus comes to his own, and, all too often, his own still do not accept him, after having 2,000 years to recognize him. It is easy to mouth the words, "I'm Catholic, I'm Christian," yet do we have room for him in the "inn" of our distracted and dissipated souls? When the dark, cold air of an egocentric culture threatens to all but choke out the fire of love and the light of truth, do we resist the currents of the times or do we go with the flow and float downstream? All too often, dead things float downstream! It takes living faith: minds animated and illumined by eternal truth and wills strengthened by grace to resist the deadly currents of a decaying society.

Mary and Joseph had gone from the town of Nazareth to Judea, to King David's town of Bethlehem in order to register for the census in compliance with the decree of Caesar Augustus. Words are of the utmost importance. After all, it was the "Word" who "became flesh and dwelt among us." The word Bethlehem signifies "house of bread." So that holy night 2,000 years ago in a town called the "house of bread," Mary gave birth to her first-born [and only] Son and wrapped him in swaddling clothes and laid him in a manger (Luke 2:7). A "manger" is a place where a higher being sets food for lower beings--we put hay in a manger for cattle or other animals.

That "silent night" God arranged that the One who would one day call himself "the Bread of

Life" (John 6:35, 6:41, 6:48, 6:51) would be born in a town called "house of bread" and laid in a place where food is made available by a higher being for lower beings. God our Father had given us the greatest gift even God could give-- the gift of his only Son, who is One with the Father and the Holy Spirit.

In the stillness of that night of nights, as the Word who had become flesh and was now dwelling among us lay safe in his mother's arms, even then the sacrifice which was the eternal Father's unalterable will was prepared. Soon enough He would suffer, die, and rise on the third day, giving himself to us the "night before He suffered" as the bread of life and the cup of eternal salvation.

The Eucharist is the greatest gift a loving God could ever give--the gift of himself. The Eucharistic Lord continues to "come to his own," and how often his own still do not accept him. The same Jesus in his entirety comes to us in the Eucharist: body, blood, soul and divinity--a real, true, and substantial presence--the highest mode of presence on earth. Do we recognize him for all that He is, or do we not recognize who it is that knocks at the door of the inn?

The Word who became flesh still dwells among us: Emmanuel--God among us--is among us indeed, on every altar and in every tabernacle of every Catholic Church in the world. We are to become one with the Eucharistic Lord Jesus and, filled with him, bring him to all the world. By living his life--a life of prayer, penance and virtue--we become who we are: the body of Christ. Glory to God in the highest, and peace to his people on earth!

Ever Ancient...Ever New

Chapter Ten
The Mystery of Christian Love

We have today a crisis of words. Words are of paramount importance, for they convey concepts. Indeed, the Son of God is the "Eternal Word" of the Father. One of the most important words in all of language is "love." Today it has become necessary to continually clarify this word and the reality which gives rise to it and supports it. We shall speak of the highest signification of the term, the Christian one.

We know that God himself is love (see the First Letter of John, especially 4:16). In order to understand love, a function of the intellect, and then to exercise it, a function of the will, we must look at this God who is love itself. We look at Jesus Christ to see the God who is love, and the way we as human persons are to exercise this love, for Jesus is true God and true man. He is the "reflection of the Father's glory, the exact representation of the Father's being" (Hebrews 1:3).

Our Lord tells us clearly that He has loved us as the Father loves him, and He desires us to live on in his love. He clarifies the point, knowing that we are slow to understand at times. "You will live in my love if you keep my commandments" (John 15:10). The New Covenant clearly did not abolish the Old Covenant; rather, it brought it to fulfillment (See Mt. 19:16-19). The Ten Commandments are still there for us, as the Catechism of the Catholic Church teaches: "Since they express man's fundamental duties toward God [love] and towards his neighbor [love], the Ten Commandments reveal, in their primordial content, grave obligations. They are fundamentally immutable, and they oblige always and everywhere. No one can dispense from them. The Ten Commandments are engraved by God in the human heart.

There has been a notion in recent years that implies that somehow the Commandments are an affront to our freedom or dignity as humans. Nothing could be further from the truth. The fact of the matter is that the infinite wisdom who is our provident and loving Father gave us the commandments to set our freedom free, and to insure we live in accordance with our human dignity.

Some of us think that the precepts laid down by God and his church are humanly impossible to keep. We cannot of our own diminished and impoverished power keep the Commandments as perfectly as the holiness of God and our creation in the image and likeness of God demands. We are in need of help to do this. We have the help. This is the reason Jesus assumed a human nature and became like one of us in everything except sin. This is the reason for the Paschal Mystery--the mystery of love.

God's grace provides the power to obey the Commandments, hence to love, and to live a truly human and truly Christian existence. God's grace provides the light to see the authentic answers to people's questionings about the meaning of love, of human life, activity, and death:

The most perfect answer to these questionings is to be found in God alone, who created man in his own image and redeemed him from sin; and this answer is given in the revelation in Christ his Son who became man. Whoever follows Christ the perfect man becomes himself more of a man (Vatican II, Gaudium et Spes, 41).

We must use the means God has given us for acquiring his grace: the seven sacraments, especially the sacraments of reconciliation and the Eucharist, prayer and penance, and the assiduous practice of all of the human and Christian virtues. If we do this the grace will be there for us, and indeed we'll have the power to love the Lord with all of our heart, mind, and strength, and to love our neighbor as ourself. Without making use of the means available, however, we should not wonder that we can't live and love as God and his church would have us do.

"Love one another as I have loved you. There is no greater love than this: to lay down one's life for one's friends. You are my friends if you do what I command you" (John 15:12-14). Authentic love involves sacrifice; it is essentially an act of the will. To imagine that love is primarily a feeling, an emotion, or a chemistry is a fatal error. This fallacious notion kills marriages before they ever come to life. If love is merely a feeling or emotion it is up one day and down the next, and that is not the kind of roller coaster ride God wills for his beloved children. Love is a decision, an act of the will. We will the highest and best thing for the sake of the beloved, even if, and especially if, it costs us dearly. That is the love of the Father. That is the love of his only Son who was sent "that whosoever would believe in him would not perish, but have eternal life." That is truly Christian and truly human love.

If we love each other as God has first loved us, we desire what God desires for us: eternal salvation. All else pales into utter insignificance when compared to this fundamental object of human existence. "If you gain the whole world, and destroy yourself in the process, what have you gained?" (See Mt 16:26, Mk 8:36, Lk 9:25). If a husband loves a wife, if a wife loves her husband, if they love their children, if a priest loves his people, etc., then they not only desire the highest and best good for the sake of those they love, but they will do anything and everything possible to bring this about. We must put on the mind of Christ, the mind of a savior. Love in the end always entails self-sacrifice.

In this age of self-assertiveness, in this day of "looking out for number one," and in an egocentric age this is a mighty challenge to be met head on by Christians. Do we love enough to embrace the cross in our life? Will we suffer any and all things in order to guard and guide those we love to paradise? Will husbands put their wives and children first? Will wives do the same? Will priests pray and do penance for their people--suffer for them? Will we embrace the cross for each other? Will we order our entire lives in the best interest of the salvation of souls, especially the souls of our own loved ones?

Living a holy and upright life involves having enough humility to obey God's Commandments and the precepts of his Church, and it involves helping others to do so as well. "The servant is no better than the Master," (See Matthew 10:24-25, John 13:16, 15:20). The Master said "where I am, there my servant will be" (See John 12:26).

It was necessary that He be "lifted up from earth" in order to "draw all men to myself" (See John 12:32). It is necessary for us to enter into the self-donating love of Christ in order to likewise draw our loved ones to Jesus, and through him to the Father.

Indeed, "There is no greater love than this: to lay down one's life for one's friends."

Chapter Eleven
Turn Away from Sin; Be Faithful to the Gospel

The holy season of Lent helps us to come into a greater awareness of reality: the reality of God's infinite love and mercy, and the reality of our urgent need of this loving mercy. We are sinners.

Indeed, as St. John the Evangelist reminds us, "If we say, 'We are free of the guilt of sin,' we deceive ourselves; the truth is not to be found in us. But if we acknowledge our sins, he who is just can be trusted to forgive our sins and cleanse us from every wrong" (1 John 1:8-9).

There are two essential parts of this truth: first, we are indeed sinners, much in need of mercy; second, God is more than ready, willing and able to forgive our sins and restore us to grace. The "Good News" is that God has indeed sent his Son that we might be liberated from the slavery of sin. The essential prerequisite of receiving God's mercy, however, is repentance. If we say we are without sin, or that some of our sinful actions are not in fact sinful, then we reject God's healing mercy.

"Turn away from sin and be faithful to the Gospel," (Mark 1:15) the priest says as he places the ashes on the forehead of the faithful. These words in effect began the active ministry of Jesus. They are likewise the essence of the message of St. John the Baptist and all the prophets, of whom Jesus is the personification and consummation of their prophetic message.

Lent is a time of mercy; a time to indeed reform our lives and be faithful to the Gospel, for indeed (as the other formula for placing the ashes on the foreheads of believers has it), "Remember, you are dust and to dust you will return."

Jesus calls each one of us to conversion. Baptism is the place of the first and fundamental conversion (Catechism #1427). Conversion is not a one-time thing, however. We are called to a constant and lifelong conversion. "It is an uninterrupted task for the whole Church who, clasping sinners to her bosom, [is] at once holy and always in need of purification, [and] follows constantly the path of penance and renewal" (Vatican II, Lumen Gentium 8:3).

Authentic penance or conversion is first and foremost interior (#1430). This interior conversion then manifests itself in the exterior works of penance such as fasting, almsgiving and prayer. As the Catechism teaches us, interior repentance is a radical reorientation of our whole life, a return, a conversion to God with all our heart, an end of sin, and a turning away from evil, with repugnance toward the evil actions we have committed. At the same time it entails the desire and resolution to change one's life, with hope in God's mercy and trust in the help of his grace (#1431).

Our interior works of penance can take many forms. Scripture and the fathers of the church insist above all on three main forms: fasting, prayer and almsgiving, which express conversion of heart in relation to oneself, to God and to others (#1434).

Pope Paul VI's Apostolic Constitution on Penance, Paenitemini (Feb. 17, 1966), is the most important immediate post-Vatican II document on penance. It reflects the Council's thought on the nature and necessity of penance. Chapter one of that document reminds us, "Therefore, following the Master, every Christian must renounce himself, take up his own cross and participate in the sufferings of Christ...Furthermore, following the Master, he can no longer live for himself, but must live for Him who loves him and gave Himself for him. He will also have to live for his brethren, completing in his flesh that which is lacking in the sufferings of Christ...for the benefit of his body, which is the Church" (Colossians 1:24).

Pope Paul VI, in the same document, declared and established among other things that, "By divine law all the faithful are required to do penance." Penance takes many forms, but the church, in the same document, insists, first of all, that the virtue of penance be exercised in persevering faithfulness to the duties of one's state in life, in the acceptance of the difficulties arising from one's work and from human coexistence, in a patient bearing of the trials of earthly life and of the utter insecurity which pervades it (Paul VI, Paenitemini, Chapter 3).

Our interior conversion of heart thus takes many concrete forms, not the least of which is living out our state of life with generous acceptance of the normal trials and tribulations which accompany it. Likewise, as the Catechism teaches us, conversion is accomplished in daily life by gestures of reconciliation, concern for the poor, the exercise and defense of justice and right, the admission of faults to one's brethren, fraternal correction, revision of life, examination of conscience, spiritual direction, acceptance of suffering, and endurance of persecution for the sake of righteousness. Taking up one's cross each day and following Jesus is the surest way of penance (#1435).

Lent is indeed a time of conversion. Our interior penance should then manifest and prove itself in the exterior works of penance. The interior and exterior dimensions of conversion and penance are not in opposition; they are complimentary, and together they comprise the integral work of authentic penance. The interior disposition leads surely to the concrete exterior works of penance, and the exterior works should give evidence of the proper interior disposition.

Concretely, during Lent we should be praying more; we should fast as our physical condition permits us prudently; and we should share what we have with others. This may take the form of almsgiving--more relevant than ever for those of us living in an affluent society, considering the degrading poverty of so many millions today. It can also mean sharing our time with the poor and needy, volunteer work in soup kitchens, hospitals, etc.

The three traditional forms of penance strengthen each other. As Scripture tells us, "a three-ply cord is not easily broken" (Ecclesiastes 4:12). Fasting strengthens our prayer and almsgiving and gives evidence of the virtue which prayer and fasting promote. This Lent, persevering faithfully in the daily duties of our state in life, may the spirit of prayer, fasting and almsgiving lead us safely and surely through the 40 days in the desert ever closer to the promised land of the Resurrection.

Chapter Twelve
The Joy of Reconciliation

During the holy season of Lent it is good for us to continually recall the great mercy of God shown us through the Passion, death, Resurrection, and Ascension of Jesus Christ. One of the greatest manifestations of this divine mercy is the sacrament of penance, reconciliation, or confession. "Those who approach the sacrament of Penance obtain pardon from God's mercy for the offense committed against him, and are, at the same time, reconciled with the Church which they have wounded by their sins and which by charity, by example, and by prayer labors for their conversion" (Catechism #1422).

There has been a most unfortunate decline in the use of the sacrament of penance in recent years. This may in part be due to what Pope Pius XII called the "sin of the century." "The sin of the century," the Holy Father told a catechetical congress meeting in the United States in 1946, "is the loss of the sense of sin" (Pius XII, Radio Address to the United States Catechetical Congress held in Boston [26 Oct., 1946: AAS Discorsi e Radiomessaggi, VIII (1946), 288]).

A balance between the horror of sin and the infinite mercy of God must be struck, of course. God's mercy far surpasses any sin, all sin; however, in order to be a recipient of God's mercy there is an essential prerequisite: repentance for the sin committed, which includes a firm purpose of amendment. Recalling the admonition of the apostle St. John: "If we say we have no sin, we deceive ourselves, and the truth is not in us" (1 Jn 1:8), we all have the need of God's mercy for we are all sinners. It is not a negative thing to recall that we have a Savior, and that He calls us all to be free in Him. Freedom from sin and its ultimate consequence: death, is the reason Jesus suffered and died and rose again for us.

As the Catechism teaches us: "Sin is before all else an offense against God, a rupture of communion with him. At the same time it damages communion with the Church. For this reason conversion entails both God's forgiveness and reconciliation with the Church, which are expressed and accomplished liturgically by the sacrament of Penance and Reconciliation" (#1440). It is truly a great thing to be reconciled with God, with the church at large, with each member of the church, and, indeed, within our own selves. This is not a negative thing, rather a highly positive one.

Jesus Christ himself instituted the sacrament of penance; it is divine in origin, not merely human. It is not something that men in the church did later, it is something that Jesus himself did while on earth. There are two Gospel texts that are usually cited for the proof of the divine institution of the sacrament: Matthew 16:19 and John 20:22-23. The church's sacred tradition and magisterial teaching throughout the ages has interpreted these passages consistently as referring to the sacrament of penance.

Sacramental confession remains the only ordinary means of the forgiveness of serious (mortal) sins after baptism (God can at times, certainly, work through extraordinary means such as perfect contrition expressed through an Act of Contrition in an emergency). There are quite simply two sides to the process: What we do, and what God does. The "acts of the penitent" express our responsibility. First, we must have contrition. Contrition is "sorrow of the soul and detestation of the sin committed, together with the resolution not to sin again" (#1451). Contrition is perfect when it arises from that true love by which God is loved above all else (especially love for the sins we're attached to). This perfect contrition remits venial sins and also obtains forgiveness of mortal sins if it includes the firm resolution to have recourse to sacramental confession as soon as possible (#1452).

Imperfect contrition is also a gift from God which is born of the realization of the ugliness of sin and fear of eternal damnation. This kind of contrition, as the name implies, is imperfect, however it suffices when elicited in the context of sacramental confession. Outside of the sacrament, however, it is not sufficient to obtain the forgiveness of mortal or grave sin (# 1453).

It is necessary for the penitent to confess to a priest all serious or mortal sins which come to consciousness after a good examination of conscience. As the Council of Trent taught, and the Catechism reaffirms: "All mortal sins of which the penitents after a diligent self-examination are conscious must be recounted by them in confession, even if they are most secret..." (# 1456). To willfully and knowingly fail to confess all mortal sins can render the entire confession invalid as it results in lack of an integral confession. Quite simply, don't hold back on God. He already knows them, and He wants us to be set free from the weight of their guilt. Some sins, especially of a sexual nature, can be embarrassing to confess. Don't hold back. As the Nike commercial says: "Just do it!" Get it over with. What a blessing to be freed by God's loving mercy from that which keeps us from full communion with Him.

Only God can forgive sin, and He wills to do so through His ministerial priest, who acts in the person of Christ in the administration of the great sacrament of God's mercy. Confession to a priest is an essential part of the sacrament of penance or confession (#1456).

Contrary to what a few theologians have held in recent years, it is entirely possible to commit a mortal sin in one act. There are three traditional elements that constitute a mortal sin: serious matter (the sin in itself), knowledge that it is a sin, and full consent of the will in the light of this knowledge. There at times can be mitigating factors such as duress, psychological problems, etc.

Absolution takes away sin, but it does not remedy all of the wounds and disorders it causes. We must make satisfaction for sin, atone or expiate for the damage we have done through sin. This begins with the penance we are to be given by the priest. It should be salutary, meaning health-giving and restorative to the soul itself, and to the church or anyone in particular who has been hurt.

Finally, the absolution itself, which can be imparted only by a validly ordained priest, must be received by the penitent. What a great blessing for both the priest and the penitent to be part of the infinite mercy of God. How loving is our Father to have given us His Son. No matter how serious or long-standing your sins, know that God's mercy is more than enough. "Though your sins be as scarlet they can be made whiter than snow, washed in the Blood of the Lamb."

Chapter Thirteen
From the Glory of the Cross
To the Glory of Easter

"Rejoice, O earth, in shining splendor, radiant in the brightness of your King! Christ has conquered! Glory fills you! Darkness vanishes for ever!" So echoes the church all around the world at the Easter vigil, as we joyously proclaim the "Exsultet." Easter is the great victory of light over darkness, good over evil, life over death, Christ Jesus over sin, Satan, and eternal death. We are indeed a "resurrection people."

The third chapter of the book of Genesis recounts the fall of man; how the pride ("you can be like gods...") that led to disobedience ("So she took some of the fruit...and gave some to her husband...") resulted in all of the pain, suffering, and death the universe has been enduring ever since.

Original sin is an essential truth of the faith (Catechism #388), for "The Church, which has the mind of Christ, knows very well that we cannot tamper with the revelation of original sin without undermining the mystery of Christ" (#389). The consequences of Adam's sin affect all humanity, and constitute the reverse side of the "Good News" of the Paschal mystery (#402). The fathers of the church referred to Jesus as the "New Adam," for as St. Paul teaches: "...as one man's trespass led to condemnation for all men, so one man's act of righteousness leads to acquittal and life for all men" (Romans 5:18).

Since the original sin mankind had been estranged from God our Father and the gates of heaven were closed. Certainly God never stops loving his creation, but we in a sense were distanced from the One we should have loved. We were in need of someone who could reconcile the fallen universe with the Creator, who had been rejected through our sins. Only God himself could effect an adequate reconciliation, and, yet, only one like us could pay the price in justice for the offense to God. So, in God's infinitely wise plan, "the Word became flesh and dwelt among us," like one of us in every way except sin.

The eternal Word, the second person of the Blessed Trinity, assumed a human nature in order to effect reconciliation with God our Father. Jesus Christ, the Son of God, became like one of us in order to overturn the reign of sin that had so enslaved the human race. As the Catechism teaches us directly from Scripture, "Man's sins, following on original sin, are punishable by death. By sending his own Son in the form of a slave, in the form of a fallen humanity, on account of sin, God 'made him to be sin who knew no sin,' so that in him we might become the righteousness of God" (#603).

The Paschal mystery is a strict unity: the Passion and death of Christ cannot be separated from the Resurrection. We are "resurrection people" because we are united under the banner of love: the cross of Christ. It is at the cross of Christ where all roads cross. The intersection of the beams of the cross is the exact point where wisdom is to be found, for there incarnate Wisdom, Jesus Christ, is "lifted up." It is there that we come to know both God and man, for Jesus the Christ is true God and true man. In this age of the "identity crisis" it is by looking long and hard at the cross that we can find out who we are as human persons, and who this mysterious God really is.

On the cross we see unfurled the infinite merciful love who is our heavenly Father, for as Jesus says, "He who has seen me has seen the Father." Likewise we see the meaning of our own mysterious life displayed for us, for Jesus is "the image of the invisible God, the first born of all creatures..." (Colossians 1:15). We are baptized into Christ, and so share in his priestly, prophetic, and kingly life and mission. "The servant is no better than the Master," the Master said, and "where I am, there my servant will be." We see in the life and mission of Jesus Christ the true and transcendent meaning of our own human life. Indeed, as the Second Vatican Council taught, "the man who follows Jesus Christ, the perfect Man, himself becomes more of a man."

Jesus Christ laid down his life that we might have true life in him. "Dying He destroyed our death, rising He restored our life, for, indeed, "There is no greater love than this: to lay down your life for one's friends" (John 15:13). It is in following Christ in his life and death of total self-sacrifice that we truly find ourselves. So many people today are lost and frightened, wandering about without a clue as to the true meaning of human existence. The world shouts its siren song of the way to glory, "Look out for #1," "Assert yourself," and "Do your own thing," but the Word whispers to our hearts of the way to real glory: "I solemnly assure you, unless the grain of wheat falls to the earth and dies, it remains just a grain of wheat. But if it dies, it produces much fruit" (John 12:24).

"On the third day He rose again from the dead." This is what we celebrate on Easter--the real, historic, physical rising of Jesus Christ from the dead. As the Catechism teaches and firmly asserts: "The mystery of Christ's resurrection is a real event, with manifestations that were historically verified, as the New Testament bears witness..." (#639). "...Christ's Resurrection cannot be interpreted as something outside the physical order, and it is impossible not to acknowledge it as an historical fact" (#643).

Two thousand years ago some said He didn't rise from the dead, after all, "that's impossible." Today some continue to say it in various ways: That it has only an allegorical meaning; it is only in the realm of signs and merely spiritual in meaning; or the disciples made it all up afterwards. However, "If Christ has not been raised [bodily, historically, and absolutely], then our preaching is in vain and your faith is in vain" (1 Corinthians 15:14).

The truth is that the Son of God suffered and died through his human nature, liberating us from the slavery to sin, Satan and death. The truth is that He rose again on the third day--bodily, historically, absolutely! The truth is that He is alive! Jesus lives, and He invites us to pass with him through darkness to light, and from death to eternal life. "The Lamb was slain, yet lives!" And we sing with the angels on this Easter vigil: "O happy fault, O necessary sin of Adam, which gained for us so great a Redeemer!

This is the night when Jesus Christ broke the chains of death and rose triumphant from the grave. Rejoice, O earth, in shining splendor, radiant in the brightness of your King! Christ has conquered! Glory fills you! Darkness vanishes for ever!

Chapter Fourteen
The Last Things:
Judgement, Heaven, Hell, Purgatory

The church, unable and unwilling to change the essential teaching of Jesus Christ, has from the beginning taught about the "last things," or "eschatology" as the subject is termed in theology: judgment (both particular and last), heaven, hell, and purgatory. With respect to these essential elements of our Catholic Christian faith we might apply the old adage: "The more things change, the more they stay the same."

The Catechism of the Catholic Church has reiterated and confirmed the traditional teaching of the church regarding these matters. There is a judgment of every human being according to the state of our soul when we pass from time to eternity. There is heaven, hell and purgatory. To deny any of these essential teachings of the Catholic faith is for a Catholic tantamount to a denial of the faith itself. In an age when tolerance has often been confused with permissiveness it is most important to assert these truths of the faith with clarity and without nuancing them into utter ambiguity.

The Catechism (Nos. 1020-1060) gives the church's basic teaching concerning these "last things." Anyone who has learned their faith well will conclude that indeed there is nothing new contained herein. A review of the basics never hurts any of us, especially when they concern our eternal destiny.

The church reminds us that, "The Christian

who unites his own death to that of Jesus views it as a step towards him and an entrance into everlasting life"(#1020).

Our Lord took the sting out of death. He met it head on, and the person who lives and dies in Christ has no need to fear death and dying. Jesus Christ won the victory for us through the Paschal Mystery. That does not, however, mean that we do nothing. We must accept the victory. How do we do it? Quite simply by living the life of Christ: a moral life lived in concert with the true and the good. How do we know what that is and how to do it? Quite simply, by accepting the church's teaching, all of it. For the church, like a good mother, teaches her children how to live and how to die in Christ.

The particular judgment is that judgment which comes immediately upon death. "Each will be rewarded immediately after death in accordance with his works and faith" (#1021). As the Catechism reminds us, and it is defined teaching, not optional: Each man receives his eternal retribution in his immortal soul at the very moment of his death, in a particular judgment that refers his life to Christ: either entrance into the blessedness of heaven--through a purification (purgatory) or immediately--or immediate and everlasting damnation (Hell) (#1022).

This statement of our faith is clear and is not to be nuanced into oblivion. Every soul ultimately ends in heaven or hell. How we live here and now determines how we shall live forever. The possibility of sinning seriously (mortal sin) is a terrifying reality. If we die without repenting, hell is the result. We do not like to think of this, much less speak of it, but it is necessary to do so.

Mercy is for now; judgment is for later. We must accept God's mercy now through repentance and the sacrament of reconciliation while there is still time.

According to the Catechism, "Those who die in God's grace and friendship and are perfectly purified (with no need of purgatory) live for ever with Christ"(Heaven) (#1023). Heaven is the ultimate end and fulfillment of the deepest human longings, the state of supreme, definitive happiness. Heaven is what we are made for. Anything less is a catastrophe, for the only definitive failure in a human life is the loss of eternal salvation. The only definitive success in a human life is sanctification and, ultimately, heaven. The way we live must reflect this most basic and compelling of truths.

Purgatory is the final purification of a person who is on their way to heaven. Only the truly pure and perfected in grace can see God face to face. If we don't achieve the perfection of charity on this earth the mercy of God provides for us a place of final purification. This is purgatory, and it is a doctrine of the faith. "The Church formulated her doctrine of faith on Purgatory especially at the Councils of Florence and Trent" (#1031). The church's teaching is based upon certain texts of Scripture such as 2 Maccabees 12:46, remembering that only the church's magisterium has the authority to authentically interpret Scripture, not any individual expressing what they think is "plausible."

Hell is a terrifying possibility. "We cannot be united with God unless we freely choose to love him" (#1033). This means we accept the life of Christ. This means we freely choose to live the moral life which the church teaches us to live. This means we form our conscience to the objective truth which is the church's teaching. Then we can follow our conscience and be sure of choosing the good and rejecting evil. This is love. It is an act of the will informed by an intellect in conformity with objective truth--God himself. Christ and his teaching are one. This is what the Church teaches. This is what sets us free. This is what propels us on a course for heaven and away from hell.

"To die in mortal sin without repenting and accepting God's merciful love means remaining separated from him for ever by our own free choice. This state of definitive self-exclusion from communion with God and the blessed is called 'hell'" (#1033). The teaching of the Church affirms the existence of Hell and its eternity. Immediately after death the souls of those who die in a state of mortal sin descend into hell, where they suffer the punishments of hell, "eternal fire." The chief punishment of hell is eternal separation from God, in whom alone man can possess the life and happiness for which he was created and for which he longs.

As Scripture teaches us, "God wills not the death of a sinner..." Rather, God wills that "all men be saved and come to the knowledge of the truth" (1 Timothy 2:4). It is up to us to responsibly exercise our freedom in the light of truth--to choose the good and reject evil. This is love, for Jesus told us clearly: "If you live according to my teaching, you are truly my disciples" (John 8:31); and, "If you wish to enter into life, keep the commandments" (Matthew 19:17); and, yet again, "He who obeys the commandments he has from me is the man who loves me" (John 14:21).

Love is a decision, an act of the will. May God grant each of us the grace to freely and intelligently choose to love him by accepting his teaching: the teaching of Jesus Christ -- the teaching of the one, holy, catholic, and apostolic Church.

Ever Ancient...Ever New

Chapter Fifteen
Human Life:
To Know and Love God

God, infinitely perfect and blessed in himself, in a plan of sheer goodness freely created man to make him share his own blessed life. For this reason, at every time and in every place, God draws close to man. He calls man to seek him, to know him, to love him with all his strength. So teaches the very first paragraph of the Catechism (CCC #1). At a time in the history of the western world when humanity so often seems to be suffering from the so-called "identity crisis," a cry needs to echo from the rooftops: Awake, arise o sleeper, ascend men and women of the universe to your full potential: Become who you are; become the living presence of Jesus Christ to this suffering world!

How often I have been asked by the people, often enough young people, Why are we alive? What is the meaning of human existence? Those of us who learned our Faith from the old Baltimore Catechism remember that the reason God created us is to know Him, to love Him and to serve Him so that we might be happy with Him forever in heaven. This may seem an over-simplification to some, yet it is absolutely true.

God created us to share his own divine life. He sent his only Son as our Lord and Savior, our Brother and our Friend, that we "might be saved and come to the knowledge of the truth" (1 Timothy 2:3-4). Jesus Christ, who is incarnate Truth, taught nothing less than himself, and "so that this call should respond throughout the world, Christ sent forth the apostles he had chosen, commissioning them to proclaim the gospel..." (CCC #2). Christ taught the Apostles, and they handed on his teaching faithfully to their successors the bishops in union with Peter's successor, the Bishop of Rome, the Pope.

Every one of us, incorporated into Christ through Baptism, has a solemn obligation to hand on faithfully what we have received through the Church. "All Christ's faithful are called to hand it on from generation to generation, by professing the faith, by living it in fraternal sharing, and by celebrating it in liturgy and prayer" (CCC #3; cf. Acts 2:42). Since we have been given the gift of the Catechism of the Catholic Church in our time, catechesis is rightly taking on a reward prominence in the formation of the People of God.

As the Catechism itself tells us (CCC #4), that name catechesis was given from early in the Church's history "to the totality of the Church's efforts to make disciples, to help men believe that Jesus is the Son of God so that believing they might have life in his name, and to educate and instruct them in this life, thus building up the body of Christ" (Cf. JPII, Catechisi Tradendae 1;2). We are much in need of an infusion of that life in his name in an era which has an obvious latent death wish. From the first moment of conception to the last moments of old age, life is under attack; from abortion to euthanasia, with suicide and all manner of violence in between, human life is truly under attack. The counterattack to this assault on life is the One who is Life itself--The Way, The Truth, and The Life--Jesus, the Christ.

Catechesis, quite simply, educates us in Christ and through Christ so that we might become everything we have been created to be: the presence of Christ through grace in the world. It is sorely needed today. The Church's own definition of catechesis is helpful: "Catechesis is an education in the faith of young children, young people and adults which includes especially in teaching of Christian doctrine imparted, generally speaking, in an organic and systematic way, with a view to initiating the hearers into the fullness of Christian life" (CCC, #5; cf.Catechesi Tradendae, 18).

Most of the misery and unhappiness in the world today is due to the undeniable fact that many do not realize that only by loving, knowing and serving God can man be happy, for only in Jesus Christ, true God and true man, can a man or woman find their true identity and purpose in life. "The desire for God is written in the human heart, because man is created by God and for God" (CCC, #27); Our hearts are restless, O Lord, until they rest in You," said St. Augustine, echoing the inmost reality of our yearning for happiness. Only in God the Father, Son and Holy Spirit can we find such true happiness.

It is through the Church's Magisterium, authentic and authoritative interpreter of God's revelation, that men and women can be certain that their concept of God is accurate and in accord with the objective reality of God's revelation of Himself to us in the Person of Jesus Christ. It was at Caesaria Phillipi that Jesus asked his followers who people say that He is (Mt. 16:13f). What He received was conflicting and contradictory responses: Some say John the Baptist, some say Elijah, or Jeremiah, or one of the prophets. He then asked them who they themselves thought He was. Only one voice rang out with the resonate note of truth, the voice of Peter: "You are the Christ, Son of the living God!" Jesus, for his part, named Peter; "You are the Rock and upon this Rock I will build my Church and the gates of hell (the very power of eternal death) will not prevail against it."

My dear friends, if you want to know Jesus Christ and his teaching, if you want to know the true face of Truth, the true identity of Christ, then look to the successor of St. Peter, the Holy Father Pope John Paul II. Do not listen to the discordant and dissident voices of the deceived who go about deceiving others. Look rather to the successor of St. Peter and the bishops united to him, the true teachers and shepherds of the flock. Then, through the gift of obedience, having ears with which to listen, you will be enabled not only to hear, but to become a part of the magnificent symphony of eternal Truth.

Chapter Sixteen
Mary: Mother of
The New Evangelization

Pope John Paul II, that great witness of the Gospel, has reminded us that "Evangelization is the most powerful and stirring challenge which the Church has been called to from her very beginning" (Veritatis splendor, 106). This flows from the mandate of Christ to "Go into all the world and preach the Gospel to the whole creation" (Mk 16:15).

There is great deal of interest in evangelization and "new evangelization" or "re-evangelization" today. Bishops, priests, religious institutes, and the lay faithful have demonstrated a genuine desire to respond positively to this challenge to evangelize and re-evangelize. However, although programs and policies have been formulated, they often fail to note the most fundamental and necessary element: the absolute necessity and prerequisite for the personal holiness of the one evangelizing (The Catechism of the Catholic Church, #2013-2014).

There is a fundamental fact of life we must acknowledge: there is only one who truly has the power to evangelize and his name is Jesus Christ. To the extent that we enter into his life and mission we become a force for imparting the Gospel to the church, and through the church to "the whole creation." As Pope Paul VI reminded us in his apostolic exhortation Evangelii nuntiandi, "Above all the Gospel must be proclaimed by witness" (#21).

To be an effective witness of the Gospel entails more "being" than "doing." First, we have to become who we are. We are created in God's image, and "the image of the invisible God, the first born of all creation" (cf. Col. 1:15) is Jesus. We, through grace, are called to become the presence of Jesus Christ in the world. There is no other authentic meaning of human existence. Indeed, "The man who follows Jesus Christ, the perfect man, himself becomes more of a man," as the Second Vatican Council teaches (The Church in the Modern World, #41).

How, then, do we personally accomplish this fundamental mission of our lives? How in a practical way can we become who we are called to be: Jesus made present to the world? We are in the month of October, the month the church has traditionally dedicated to the rosary of the Virgin Mary. And here we have the answer: Mary, mother of the Lord, mother of the church, spiritual mother of each and every Christian. Mary shows us the way to her Son, the one who is "the Way, the Truth, and the Life."

It was through the faith and fiat of Mary and the creative artistry of the Holy Spirit, "the Lord and the giver of life," that Life himself was conceived and brought forth in accordance with the Father's perfect and holy will. This same essential dynamism goes on as the Body of Christ is conceived mystically and brought forth in her members.

Authentic Marian devotion, which is Christocentric, and doctrinal in its foundation, will lead a person into this mystery of Jesus Christ (#964). It can help us to enter into the life and mission of Jesus Christ, and this is the only possible way each one of us can be an effective instrument for the "new evangelization." Mary shows us how to "become like little children" in the one who is the only Son of the Father. She is the Father's perfect daughter: docile, humble, faithful, obedient to his will, on fire with love even as far as the cross. In desiring to fulfill the Father's will we say fiat to the Father's most holy will: "Yes, Lord, here I am, come to do your will."

Mary, although at the Annunciation she didn't understand it all, "How can this be...?", rendered the obedience of faith: "Be it done unto me according to your word...And the Word became flesh and dwelt among us." We, like Mary, are called to give the assent of faith: to believe in God; to believe all that God has said and revealed to us, and to believe all that holy church proposes for our belief because He is truth itself (#1814). In accepting the revelation of God as interpreted authentically and authoritatively by the church's magisterium we bring forth Christ in the world.

In her childlike simplicity and humility Mary becomes perfectly open to the action of the Holy Spirit--the "Lord and the giver of life" as the Nicene Creed calls him. He overshadows her and she becomes his spouse, conceiving the One who is Life itself. Hence, Mary, perfectly obedient to the Father's will, and perfectly receptive to the action of the Holy Spirit, conceives and brings forth the One who is "Way, Truth, and Life" in a world that had lost its way, "exchanged the truth of God for a lie," and rejected life in favor of sin which leads to death ("the wages of sin is death" {Cf. Rom. 6:23).

Mary is the mother par excellence, for she is the mother of God (#495). This God, who is also true man, gave her to us from the cross in the person of his beloved disciple, St. John. As mother of the church Mary continues to fulfill a mother's function (#963). A mother is one who says "yes" to life; one who conceives life and gives it the light of day. She then brings that life to maturity by nurturing it: feeding and educating her children. October is a good time to begin actively praying the rosary for the success of the new evangelization, since that success begins with each of us individually. The rosary is nothing less than the prayer of the Gospels. The Gospel is what evangelization is all about. As we pray the rosary we meditate upon the 15 mysteries, 13 of which are found explicitly in the Gospels, two of which can be deduced from the Scriptures.

The main prayers of the "Our Father" and "Hail Mary" are gospel prayers. We begin to interiorize the Gospel, which means we begin to interiorize Jesus Christ, who is the "Good News" of the Gospel. We thus begin to become who we are. In becoming the living presence of Jesus, "the Light of the world," we also become light for a world sinking into darkness under the weight of its own iniquity.

In this way we become a powerful force for the "new evangelization", and, like St. Paul, we can cry out with joy: "It is no longer I who live, but Christ who lives within me!" (Cf. Gal. 2:20).

Chapter Seventeen
The Eucharist as a
Sacrifice of Thanksgiving

Both the Catechism and the Second Vatican Council teach that the Eucharist is "the source and summit of the Christian life. The other sacraments, and indeed all ecclesiastical ministries and works of the apostolate, are bound up with the Eucharist and are oriented toward it. For in the blessed Eucharist is contained the whole spiritual good of the church, namely Christ himself, our Pasch." (#1324).

The holy Eucharist is so essential that the church asserts: "In brief, the Eucharist is the sum and the summary of our faith: 'Our way of thinking is attuned to the Eucharist, and the Eucharist in turn confirms our way of thinking'" (#1327).

This being the case, it behooves us to have a very clear understanding of the church's basic teaching concerning the sacrament of sacraments in which "the whole spiritual good of the church is contained."

The term Eucharist is used because it is an action of thanksgiving to God. The Greek words eucharistein and eulogein recall the Jewish blessings that proclaim, especially during a meal, God's great works of creation, redemption and sanctification (#1328).

The greatest, and actually the only absolutely efficacious (thanks to the Father), is the total loving sacrifice of the only Son, the Lord Jesus on the cross. The Eucharist is often, and rightly, called the Holy Sacrifice of the Mass. It is holy because it is the sacrifice of the only one who with the Father and the Holy Spirit is holy, holiness personified: Jesus the Christ, a divine subject of action. It is offered in the power of the Holy Spirit, the one called the sanctifier, to the all-holy Father. To the degree that we enter into the life and mission of this triune God we are sanctified. Conformity to Jesus Christ, an action of the Holy Spirit, is what makes us pleasing to the Father, giving him perfect thanks and praise.

The Eucharist is a true sacrifice, the very same one-only sacrifice of Christ on the cross, offered in an unbloody manner to the Father in expiation of the sins of the world. We do not repeat this sacrifice because it was offered once for all. We enter into it and make it present. Only the God who transcends time and space can do such a thing, and Jesus Christ, at once the high priest and the Lamb of God who takes away the sins of the world, is the subject effecting such a marvelous transaction.

The ministerial priest in virtue of the sacrament of holy orders is the instrument of the high priest's action at the holy sacrifice. It is the Father's will that this saving action be effected, for He is the first and ultimately efficacious cause of all things. He works through his only Son, the high priest and perfect victim, and the Holy Spirit, both of whom He has sent on the mission of redemption and sanctification; the mission of redemption appropriated to the Son, sanctification to the Holy Spirit. Hence, the holy sacrifice of the Mass is an action of the Holy Trinity, as are all works ad extra (outside of the interior operation of the Trinity) of God, but not only of the Trinity. God unites himself with man, and indeed all of creation, to effect this consummately saving and sanctifying action.

The Eucharist is a true sacrifice because it represents (makes present) the one-only sacrifice of the cross, because it is its memorial, and because it applies its fruit (#1366). As the Catechism further teaches, the sacrifice of Christ on the cross and the sacrifice of the Eucharist are one single sacrifice: "The Victim is one and the same: the same now offers through the ministry of priests, who then offered himself on the Cross; only the manner of offering is different" (#1367).

We know that Christ and his church are one. The analogy is of the bride and bridegroom in a marriage. Jesus is the groom, the Church his mystical bride. "The two become one flesh" as it were. Christ come to full stature is Jesus the head of his mystical body and the church, his body, working as one. "Where I am, there my servant will be," the Master says. "It is necessary that I be lifted up in order to draw all men to myself," Jesus likewise asserted, referring to the sacrifice of the cross. Each member of the body of Christ, and the body as a whole, walk the way of sacrifice if we are to be authentic members of Christ. His way (the One who said "I am the way") is our way. Good Friday always precedes Easter Sunday on my liturgical calendar. In order to enjoy the glory we must endure, indeed even joyfully, the sacrifice. In other words, "No pain, no gain; no cross, no crown; no gall no glory!"

Hence, "the Eucharist is also the sacrifice of the church," as the church herself teaches: "The Church which is the Body of Christ participates in the offering of her Head. With him, she herself is offered whole and entire. She unites herself to his intercession with the Father for all men. In the Eucharist the sacrifice of Christ becomes also the sacrifice of the members of his Body. The lives of the faithful, their praise, sufferings, prayer, and work, are united with those of Christ and with his total offering, and so acquire a new value. Christ's sacrifice present on the altar makes it possible for all generations of Christians to be united with his offering" (#1368).

The term "Mass" (Missa) is still appropriately used for the Eucharistic sacrifice, "because," as the Catechism teaches, "the liturgy in which the mystery of salvation is accomplished concludes with the sending forth (missio) of the faithful, so that they may fulfill God's will in their daily lives" (#1332).

Each time we participate in the Eucharist, the holy sacrifice of the Mass, we enter mystically into the mission of the Lord Jesus Christ, which is redemption, and the way He accomplished the mission, which is on a cross oriented toward resurrection. "Dying He destroyed our death, rising He restored our life," we pray at Mass. What a great joy to know that God in his infinite goodness allows us to participate in the saving work of his Son, that we can offer the joys and the pains of this life in union with Jesus crucified and risen at the Eucharistic sacrifice.

As the wonderful religious sisters who used to teach us in grammar school would say, "Place yourself on the paten and in the chalice with Jesus at Mass that you might be offered to the Father through, with, and in Jesus as a sacrifice of thanksgiving for the salvation of souls and the glory of the kingdom." It is good advice, theologically correct and, hence, pleasing to God.

Chapter Eighteen
The Laity in the Church:
A Sleeping Giant

For altogether too many years we have been rather conditioned to think of only priests and religious when we think about vocations. The fact of the matter is that each person has a vocation, a "call" from God.

The vast majority of Christians are called to the lay state, so a knowledge of what this common, yet immensely noble and holy, state of life entails is essential. The Catechism (#897) tells us that: "The term 'laity' is here understood to mean all the faithful except those in Holy Orders and those who belong to a religious state approved by the Church. That is, the faithful, who by baptism are incorporated into Christ and integrated into the People of God, are made sharers in their particular way in the priestly, prophetic, and kingly office of Christ, and have their own part to play in the mission of the whole Christian people in the Church and in the world (See Vatican II, Lumen Gentium, #31).

The lay faithful are the front-line troops in the never ending moral combat to promote the true and the good. One of the most erroneous and subtly dangerous ideas ever is that somehow our religion and any and everything else in life should remain separate. A Catholic must live, witness, and, yes, vote, a well-formed Catholic conscience. The Second Vatican Council's 16 major documents refer to "conscience" 72 times, but never without a modifying term: "well-formed conscience," "mal-formed conscience", etc. As Catholics we have a serious moral obligation to form our consciences in accord with the objective and absolute norm of truth--that is, church teaching. This is quite simply another way of saying "put on the mind of Christ." One of the primary reasons that our country has largely become a moral wasteland is that we Catholics have done a dismally poor job of both forming our consciences and then living, teaching, and voting in accordance with them.

Abortion, artificial contraception, pornography, and all types of disordered lifestyles-- which are not "alternative," but rather humanly and morally degenerative and destructive, could never exist in this once great country if the Catholic lay faithful were witnessing their faith powerfully and without compromise. This is never an excuse for persecution of any group, yet love desires what is best for the beloved--and this can never be immoral behavior.

Morality is not a subjective construct. Rather, it is inscribed in the heart and mind of every person. It is our business to accept our noble and holy lot as persons, and to act in accord with nature, not rebel against it. We run the risk today in our once largely Christian country of falling into that class of idolaters which St. Paul bitterly denounced because of their refusal to worship God and accept his teaching, despite their knowledge of him (See Romans 1:20-27).

As the old saying goes, "the more things change, the more they stay the same." The Holy Spirit, speaking through St. Paul, makes it pretty clear. Catholics today in the United States represent the single largest religious voting block in the country, yet we have had relatively little effect in recent years. The reason is that an enormous number of Catholics are not faithful to their lay state in life.

The Catechism (#898) teaches, echoing Vatican II, that: "By reason of their special vocation it belongs to the laity to seek the kingdom of God by engaging in temporal affairs and directing them according to God's will...It pertains to them in a special way so to illuminate and order all temporal things with which they are closely associated that these may always be effected and grow according to Christ and may be to the glory of the Creator and Redeemer" (See Vatican II, Lumen Gentium 31, 2).

In many ways this is, and should be, an age of the laity, an age wherein a great and noble vocation receives the attention, study, and nurturing it should; but, with an increase of knowledge comes an increase of responsibility. The church clearly teaches that: "The initiative of lay Christians is necessary especially when the matter involves discovering or inventing the means for permeating social, political, and economic realities with the demands of Christian doctrine and life. This initiative is a normal element of the life of the Church (#899).

We are not to be confused by empty rhetoric and the fallacy of what is "politically correct," especially when that is largely determined by the mind of a culture which will go down in history as grandly technological, yet singularly irrational; able to travel far into outer space, yet amazingly crippled in its ability to travel inwardly in order to be in touch with the high and lofty demands of its own moral nature. We should be mightily wary of a culture, rightly described as a "culture of death," that seeks to tell us how to live, imposing laws that are illicit and mores that are immoral.

If Catholics don't begin to form their consciences to the objective and absolute norm of Truth--Church teaching in faith and morals--and then live, witness, and vote that well-formed conscience, then, we may indeed find that this culture and this country will indeed, "end with a whimper, rather than a bang." For, "evil will indeed triumph if good men remain silent." For, having once-too-often called the truth a lie and lies the truth, having repeatedly asserted that the good is evil, and evil is good, life will cease. For this once great country, which was originally founded upon transcendent and immutable Christian principles and morals, having perverted itself into a state of terminal moral cancer, having contracepted itself into sterility and aborted itself into oblivion, will simply keel over and die--another wreck on the reefs of time. It is inevitable, unless we Catholics live, witness, and vote what we profess!

Chapter Nineteen
The Holy Spirit:
Life-Giving Breath of God

"No one can say 'Jesus is Lord' except by the Holy Spirit" (1 Cor 12:3). As the Catechism reminds us, "To be in touch with Christ, we must first have been touched by the Holy Spirit...He comes to meet us and kindles faith in us" (#683). The great father of the church, St. Irenaeus, beautifully expresses the work of the blessed Trinity in our lives: "Baptism gives us the grace of new birth in God the Father, through his Son, in the Holy Spirit. For those who bear God's Spirit are led to the Word, that is, to the Son, and the Son presents them to the Father, and the Father confers incorruptibility on them. And it is impossible to see God's Son without the Spirit, and no one can approach the Father without the Son, for the knowledge of the Father is the Son, and the knowledge of God's Son is obtained through the Holy Spirit" (#683).

The Catechism reminds us that "The Church, a communion living in the faith of the apostles which she transmits, is the place where we know the Holy Spirit." At times persons, claiming to be led by the Holy Spirit, walk down spiritual roads which prove to be dead ends. The Holy Spirit works within the church and for the church, never opposed to the church's teaching and authentic life. We know the Holy Spirit: "In the Scriptures which He inspired; in the Tradition, to which the Church Fathers are always timely witnesses; in the Church's Magisterium, which

He assists; in the sacramental liturgy, through its words and symbols, in which the Holy Spirit puts us into communion with Christ; in prayer, wherein He intercedes for us; in the charisms and ministries by which the Church is built up; in the signs of apostolic and missionary life; and in the witness of saints through whom He manifests his holiness and continues the work of salvation" (#688).

The heavenly Father sends his Son and the Holy Spirit on a joint mission (#689) to gather all of his children into one in his church, the mystical Body of Christ, which has the Holy Spirit, the sanctifier, as her very soul. The soul is the principle of life, the animating force, of a body, so too with the church: the very life of the church is the Holy Spirit. The same Spirit or breath of God (Ruah Hakodesh) that moved over the waters at creation, manifested himself at the waters of the Jordan, when life himself was baptized by St. John the Baptist, thus baptizing the waters of baptism. This same Spirit of life, through Jesus, gives new life to all who accept baptism and then strive to live it.

The Father anoints his only Son with the anointing who is the Holy Spirit. The members of Christ's body, the church, are likewise in Christ anointed with the Holy Spirit through the sacraments. Anointing with oil is the sense perceptible sign of this anointing with the Holy Spirit, especially in baptism, confirmation, and holy orders. Likewise, in serious illness the "anointing of the sick" is given to strengthen us. It is the Holy Spirit who strengthens the members of Christ's body.

The "Lord and Giver of Life," as the Nicene

Creed refers to the Holy Spirit, overshadowed Mary, the all-holy ever-virgin mother of God, and "the Word became flesh and dwelt among us." Through the fiat of Mary and the action of the "Lord and Giver of Life", the Father's Son, was conceived and brought forth in time and space. "Mary...is the masterwork of the mission of the Son and the Spirit in the fullness of time" (#721).

"In Mary, the Holy Spirit fulfills the plan of the Father's loving goodness" (#723). "The Holy Spirit prepared Mary by his grace. It was fitting that the mother of him in whom 'the whole fullness of deity dwells bodily' should herself be 'full of grace (#722).'" As the Catechism goes on to tell us, "With and through the Holy Spirit, the Virgin conceives and gives birth to the Son of God. By the Holy Spirit's power and her faith, her virginity became uniquely fruitful" (#723). Mary's fruitful virginity is the exemplar and prototype of the spiritual fruitfulness of consecrated virginity and celibacy in the church. It is a charism that begets spiritual life in the Body of Christ, given by the "Lord and Giver of Life;" something to be treasured, nurtured, and safeguarded in and by the same church.

The sending of the Holy Spirit takes place only after the "going forth" of Jesus via the cross. Only when the time for his glorification has arrived does the eternal Word promise this Spirit of truth, this new paraclete. As the Catechism beautifully summarizes for us: "The Spirit of Truth, the other Paraclete, will be given by the Father in answer to Jesus' prayer; he will be sent by the Father in Jesus' name; and Jesus will send him from the Father's side, since he comes from the Father. The Holy Spirit will come and we shall know him; he will be with us forever; he will remain with us. Spirit will teach us everything, remind us of all that Christ said to us and bear witness to him. The Holy Spirit will lead us into all truth and will glorify Christ. He will prove the world wrong about sin, righteousness, and judgment" (#729).

The Holy Spirit, the third person of the blessed Trinity, carries on the mission of the Father's Son in the church. As the very soul of the church, the Spirit breathes life into the church and each of her members. We should strive to enter into a real relationship with each of the persons of the Trinity. Invoking the Holy Spirit, asking for his guidance, before doing just about anything of importance is the spiritually intelligent thing to do. Praying for the gifts of wisdom, knowledge, understanding, counsel, fortitude, piety and fear of the Lord is something that will prove fruitful for us, in order that we then may bear fruit that endures.

Chapter Twenty
Matrimony: Sacrament of Unity And Fruitful Love

The fifth chapter of St. Paul's Letter to the Ephesians is a great Magna Carta on the beautiful sacrament of matrimony. The Apostle to the Gentiles reminds wives that they should relate to their husbands as if to the Lord (In the original Greek there is no word for submissive, which is the word used in some translations). It goes on, "Husbands, love your wives, as Christ loved the church. He gave himself up for her to make her holy, purifying her..."

I have from time to time been asked by pastor friends (both Catholic and Protestant) to speak to couples who were preparing for marriage. I always take a very simple approach. After all, if people can't understand what you are talking about that isn't very "pastoral." The initial conversation goes something like this: "So, you're going to be married; Wonderful! You must be in love?"

The groom to-be might say, "Yes, sure father, of course, we're in love."

"Great! Could you please explain to me what love is in your own words?"

"Oh, you know, father, feelings, I have feelings for her."

I smile, "No, love is not merely feelings. Feelings are up and down and all around. Try again."

"It's chemistry, father, we've got great chemistry!"

I smile again. "No, love is not merely chemistry. Someday you might mix the wrong emotions together and the whole thing could blow up."

I try to help them out: "Would you say that people who are in love desire the highest and best thing for the sake of the one they love?"

"Yes, that's it, father!"

"Great," I respond, "What would you like for each other?"

"Well," the blushing bride might respond, "good health, a nice house, job security, some children, two cars, and a VCR."

"Those are all fine things. What else?" I ask.

"What else? What else is there, father?"

Now, you must understand I am speaking with Christians who have hopefully had some education in their faith. They have been secularized! They think on a purely natural plane, which is surely not enough for a Christian and a Catholic.

I always ask them when they say, "What else could there be?"

"How about heaven? How about eternal beatitude? How about being together forever with God and all of the angels and saints?"

"Oh yes, we never thought about that."

Well we'd better start thinking about it. Life is largely a waste of time if we do not have a transcendent and spiritual way of thinking. God is our origin. God is the meaning of life. God is the object and end of human life. The old Baltimore Catechism used to ask us "Why did God create us?" How well some of us might remember answering: "God created us that we might know him, love him, and serve him that we might be happy with him in heaven for all eternity."

It's that simple! That is the meaning of life in general, and that is the fundamental purpose of marriage. To forget that, or to, in the name of a more enlightened understanding or sophisticated theology, nuance that ray of pure light into utter ambiguity is not wise and it is not pastoral. As the Catechism teaches:

"The matrimonial covenant, by which a man and a woman establish between themselves a partnership of the whole of life, is by its nature ordered toward the good of the spouses and the procreation and education of offspring...(#1601).

The greatest good for any human person is eternal beatitude. This is why our loving Father created us, redeemed us through his Son, and sanctifies us through the Holy Spirit. To remember this always and to apply it in daily life is wisdom. To forget it is not.

Husband and wife must make a decision, and this is the essence of authentic love: it is a decision, an act of the will, not mere feelings. Feelings are part of it, but not the essential part. Feelings come and go. We must decide to love, "in sickness and in health, for better or for worse, rich or poor, until death do we part..." We may well not feel like it at any point on the journey, but to remain faithful is a decision. To will to sacrifice oneself for the sanctification of one's spouse and children is a decision--it is true love.

Jesus "gave himself up for her [his bride the Church] to make her holy..." (Ephesians 5:25-26). A husband and a wife must be willing to sacrifice themselves for each other. Once they exchange consent and a valid marriage comes into being it is indissoluble. Only death can dissolve the bond, assuming that it is in fact a valid marriage. Imagine if the Lord Jesus one day decided that he'd had enough of our infidelity and walked out on us. He is the bridegroom, and we as church are his mystical bride. He is faithful forever (See #1614-15).

The total self-giving necessity in marriage must be mutual obviously, or it doesn't work. It must be constant and faithful, and it is fruitful. Love is fruitful. Only in heaven will we know how magnificent, how holy, how beautiful is the reality of being a mother and father. Children are a gift. "By its very nature the institution of marriage and married love is ordered to the procreation and education of the offspring and it is in them that it finds its crowning glory" (#1652).

To enter together into the sanctuary of God's own creative power is an incalculable blessing. To bring into existence children who will never die; from the moment of conception they are destined to love and praise God forever. What a privilege! How God must love moms and dads who say "yes" to life and give Him children! Husbands and wives, mothers and fathers, your place in Heaven will be very high! Love each other. Support each other. Will to help each other and your children to "run the race to the finish line," all the way to our real goal: heaven!

Chapter Twenty One
Angels and Demons
Facts, NOT Fiction

There have been a number of television shows, movies and various articles on the subject of angels and the demonic in recent years. Most of this material is pure fiction, yet the part that is not fiction is an acknowledgment that they both exist.

As part of the church's catechesis on creation it is necessary to speak of both the angels and the devil, Satan, or the demonic. "The Apostles' Creed professes that God is the 'Creator of heaven and earth.' The Nicene Creed makes it explicit that this profession includes 'all that is, seen and unseen" (Catechism #325).

"The profession of faith of the Fourth Lateran Council (1215) affirms that God from the beginning of time made at once (simul) out of nothing both orders of creatures, the spiritual and the corporeal, that is, the angelic and the earthly, and then (deinde) the human creature, who as it were shares in both orders, being composed of spirit and body" (#327).

The Catechism clearly asserts that "the existence of the spiritual, non-corporeal beings that Sacred Scripture usually calls 'angels' is a truth of the faith" (#328), the witness of Scripture being as unanimous as tradition. In other words, there is no question about it: the angels are real, not the figment of someone's medieval imagination. It is a truth of the faith. This quite simply means that for a Catholic, one must accept this as part of God's revelation. One may not understand it, but one must accept it on faith, and then seek the understanding that faith can ultimately bring. Although, it being understood, that we'll never understand in this life God and all his mighty works perfectly. We would have to be God to understand him perfectly.

The angels are creatures, pure spiritual beings whose mission or office is to be messengers and servants of God (#329). "As purely spiritual creatures angels have intelligence and will: they are personal and immortal creatures, surpassing in perfection all visible creatures, [with the exception of the Mother of God] as the splendor of their glory bears witness" (#330).

The Lord Jesus Christ is the author, center, and end of all creation including the angelic world. They are "his angels." As the Catechism teaches, "they belong to him because they were created through and for him...They belong to him still more because he has made them messengers of his saving plan" (#331).

The existence and activity of the angels is more than obvious in both the Old and New Testaments. To say, by the way, that they are mere "literary figures" in Scripture in the name of so-called biblical scholarship is an affront to and an attack upon true scholarship. All Scripture has to be read as a totality, in the light of tradition, and applying the analogy of faith. When this is done it is clear that the church's teaching is constant in that angels are real beings, not mere literary devices. They have played a key role in salvation history:

"Angels have been present since creation...They closed the earthly paradise;

protected Lot; saved Hagar and her child; stayed Abraham's hand; communicated the law...led the People of God; announced birth's and callings; assisted the prophets...; the Angel Gabriel announced the birth of the Precursor and that of Jesus himself (#332).

"From the Incarnation to the Ascension, the life of the Word incarnate is surrounded by the adoration and service of angels...[They announced his birth to the poor shepherds];...they protect Jesus in his infancy, serve him in the desert, strengthen him in his agony in the garden...It is the angels who evangelize' by proclaiming the Good News of Christ's Incarnation and Resurrection. They will be present at Christ's return, which they will announce, to serve at his judgment (# 333).

These events wherein the angels exercised their ministry as messengers and servants of the Lord are real, as the church asserts. The entire life of the church, the mystical body of Christ, is likewise aided and benefited by the mysterious and powerful help of the angels (#334).

In addition, each and every person benefits from the ministry of the angels. The church has long taught that we have a "guardian angel" to guide and protect us through life. "From infancy to death human life is surrounded by their (the angels') watchful care and intercession. Beside each believer stands an angel as protector and shepherd leading him to life." Already here on earth the Christian life shares by faith in the blessed company of angels and men united in God.

The existence and malevolent activity of the devil or Satan and the fallen angels or demons is likewise a teaching of the church that must be accepted by all. "The Church teaches that Satan was at first a good angel, made by God: The devil and the other demons were indeed created naturally good by God, but they became evil by their own doing (#391).

Through the misuse of the gifts of intellect and free will the devil (Lucifer) and those who went his way chose irrevocably to reject God and his reign. Their choice is irrevocable because of their higher nature. Men get a second chance, and many more than that, but the angels clearly saw what they were doing. Hence, "There is no repentance for the angels after their fall, just as there is no repentance for men after death" (#393).

Christ came to cast out the evil one and his works of lying and death, and did so through the humble obedience which led him always to accept the Father's will, even unto the death of the cross. The essence of the diabolic is that pride and arrogance which leads to disobedience. This leads to fracturing and division. Stepping outside of the truth who is God himself results in this division.

Those who are most powerful in Christ through his church, which is called to fight against "the liar and father of lies, the murderer from the beginning" (cf.. Jn 8:42f) (the devil), are those who are most humbly obedient to God's authority working through the church. The devil can do nothing when he comes up against those who obey most humbly Christ's church and her teachings. On the other hand, he is most powerful and untiringly active working through those who imagine themselves to be above the church's teaching authority. Humility leads to obedience, which leads to life. Pride leads to disobedience, which leads to death. This is the lesson of the book of Genesis. It is the lesson of the cross.

With the angels of the Lord we humbly and obediently praise and give thanks to the Father through Christ in the power of the Holy Spirit for all that God's creative and redemptive power has wrought.

Chapter Twenty Two
On The Passing of
John Paul the Great

A great athlete has run his last race. A great teacher has taught his final class. A great poet has lived his greatest masterpiece. A great warrior has fought his last battle. Pope John Paul II has died. In his life and in his death he has, however, left us a rich legacy.

The first time I remember thinking of him as John Paul the Great was in seminary in the late 1980s. The Director of Priestly Formation, a good priest and scholar, Fr. David Liptak, used to regularly speak of the Holy Father in those terms, both to us, and in his newspaper columns in the Archdiocese of Hartford's newspaper. There were few of us who wouldn't have agreed with him, then and now.

The Holy Father's gifts and accomplishments are too many to enumerate here. That has been done and will be done for years to come.

What is his greatest accomplishment? What did he teach us that was most important? Everyone will have their own ideas about it. I'll tell you mine, since everyone else these days are telling us theirs, as it should be.

Pope John Paul II was a contemplative in action. He taught us, more than anything else, that prayer really is the soul of the apostolate. His prodigious accomplishments in the ecclesial, as well as the secular sphere, were enabled and empowered by the force of his interior life. He was a man of prayer, a man of deep contemplative prayer. He was a Carmelite at heart, and he had learned his lessons well from the great doctors of prayer, St. Teresa of Avila and St. John of the Cross, among others.

He knew that the true purpose of human existence is union with God: Father, Son, and Holy Spirit. The Holy Spirit, a divine artist, sculpting Christ within us unto the glory of God our Father. One must be well disposed, malleable, and open to the action of grace for this to take place. Humility is the key that opens the door to the treasure room of such grace. John Paul was an incredibly gifted man, and an incredibly humble man.

All of the strength and power that impelled him around the world several times over, all of the intellectual and spiritual energy that enabled him to write encyclical after encyclical and apostolic letter after apostolic letter came from his union with God. It was this union, effected through an intense life of prayer, that gave him the grace that, building on his nature, left aides and reporters gasping for breath trying to keep up with him all those years.

He had a deep, simple devotion and relationship with the Blessed Virgin Mary. She walked with him every step of his life, from the early years when he painfully lost his own mother, then his brother, and his father. This good Mother was always with him in his darkest moments. She drew him gradually and inexorably into conformity with her Son, Jesus Christ. It was his oneness with Jesus, and Him crucified, that enabled Karol Wojtyla to soar to the greatest heights of human and Christian achievement.

Mary led him to draw close to Jesus in the holy Eucharist. He spent many hours with his Lord in the Blessed Sacrament. Every day the celebration of Mass and adoration and prayer filled him with the power he needed to be what God needed him to be for the Church and the world at a decisive moment in history.

We know his greatness in virtue of his accomplishments, for surely you can tell the tree by its fruit. The amount of good fruit from this son of Poland and the Church is astounding, and inspiring, to behold.

It is one thing to know the tree by the fruit, but what enabled the tree to grow as it did. It was prayer, and when I say prayer I do not mean merely vocal prayer, although that is very essential. I mean a life rooted in virtue, a life spent discerning and doing God's will, rather than one's own. A life that in the end must be a crucified life, a life spent in service of others. This sounds like much less than it is. To keep going when you are so tired you cannot hardly keep your eyes open, to keep going in the face of criticism and rejection, to keep going "in season and out of season, convenient or inconvenient." This is what saints do: they exercise heroic virtue. Heroic virtue, more than anything, is how the Church determines if one deserves the honor of canonization.

Pope John Paul II was given to us as a great gift by God at a decisive moment in history, both for the Church and the world. He accomplished many things, but one must reason from the effects (the fruit) back to the cause in order to truly discern the greatest lesson to be learned from his life.

His life of great active achievement was enabled and empowered by his intense life of prayer. John Paul II was a contemplative in action. Like his beloved daughter and friend, Mother Teresa of Calcutta, he knew that the source of all apostolic fruitfulness and accomplishment is a life rooted in prayer, a life so one with Jesus Christ that he would have to cry out with St. Paul, "It is no longer I who live, but Christ who lives within me...I live, and move, and have my being in Christ."

This is the lesson, the true lesson, we must take with us as we say goodbye to our Holy Father. The greatest tribute we can pay to him is to live as he lived. Live a life close to Mary, praying the Rosary each day as John Paul II did, drawing close to Jesus in the Eucharist. Become one with the Lord and through the power of His Spirit allow Him to do great things through you.

Trust, trust with all your heart, that Jesus will empower you to achieve great things the same way He enabled a humble polish laborer, Karol Wojtyla, to rise to the heights as one of the greatest popes and greatest men of all time.

Praised be Jesus Christ!

Ever Ancient...Ever New

TO ORDER MORE
COPIES OF THIS BOOK

OR TO SEE A COMPLETE CATALOG OF
FATHER CORAPI'S MATERIAL;
BOOKS, CDS, DVDS, ETC.
GO TO:
www.fathercorapi.com

OR
CALL TOLL FREE
1-888-800-7084

OR
US MAIL
SANTA CRUZ MEDIA, INC
PO BOX 550
WHITEFISH, MT, 59937